Anisa

LETTERS TO A
YOUNG
GENERATION

www.910publishing.com

LETTERS TO A YOUNG GENERATION

COMPILED BY

AMANDA WILSON

9:10 PUBLISHING

LETTERS TO A YOUNG GENERATION 2
A 9:10 Publishing Book 978-0-9571367-6-2

This edition published in 2015

Copyright © 2015 9:10 Publishing Ltd.
Selection copyright © 2015 Amanda Wilson
Foreword copyright © Kanya King and Angie Greaves
Copyright of photographs and letters has been
retained by the individual contributors
Cover and interior design © Rachel Lawston at
Lawston Design, www.lawstondesign.com

9:10 Publishing Ltd is Registered in England and Wales
Company No. 07979071
www.910publishing.com

A CIP catalogue record for this book is available
from the British Library.

Printed and bound in Great Britain by
Marston Book Services Ltd.
www.marston.co.uk

CONTENTS

To Rianna
Always remember who you are
and whose you are!

FOREWORD

The messages and lessons in this book are so surreal; kind of reminiscent of my own travels in life. I was completely drawn into each letter and story, as they serve as a testament to the phenomenal accolades women can achieve in society. I urge young females across the nation to read this book, as it inspires you to go out and grab the world by the lapels. Anyone, I mean, everyone, should be able to find a remnant of themselves within these pages.

Kanya King

I would like to start this Foreword by saying a massive Thank You to Amanda Wilson and the 9:10 Publishing Team for asking me to be involved in this project.

One of my regular quotes that I stand by is, "God plays a worldwide game of chess and being put in checkmate by Him means YOU have won the game!"

When my daughters, Morggan and Kamarane were little they used to laugh at me whenever I said that to them. But now as teenagers they see the full picture and understand the statement.

Some months ago 9:10 Publishing sent me an email asking if I could contribute a letter to this book. Unfortunately the email mysteriously went somewhere into cyberspace and away from my memory.

Whilst I would have completed the mission with vigour and passion, there was a reason why the request re-positioned its place in my mind. Weeks later, a colleague who knows my passion for books sent me a message on Twitter regarding the boys' edition of *Letters to a Young Generation*. I emailed 9:10 Publishing immediately and received a swift response together with the copy of the original email that was sent to me. After feeling a little embarrassed I realised that this was the part I was meant to play in this project.

So there you have it, checkmate. Not only is the game over, it's also a win-win situation, as now I have been given the opportunity to write the foreword for the girls' edition of *Letters to a Young Generation*.

So ladies, young ladies, what I share with you is the result of many experiences, which were not always happy but, which I now recognise were avenues that needed to be entered in order to learn valuable life lessons. I'm sure that whatever age you currently are you've had a lesson of some description. If you didn't understand that lesson you could never pass the test at the end, and therefore would need to re-take the class. The same principal applies with lessons in life, perhaps compare the situation to a driving test; you need to keep re-taking the test until you pass and are able to drive alone without supervision. Life will present these lessons until you finally learn and can then move on and grow.

Being a radio presenter is fabulous. Short working hours and a recent change meant that I was able to spend mornings with my family and also be home in time to have evenings with my family. However, there have been times over the years that I've thought about hanging up my headphones and doing something different. But whenever those feeling arose, an opportunity always presented itself that required the gift of communication that I believe I have been blessed with; little nudges of confirmation that I was in the right place and so the road and the experiences continue.

Young ladies, you have a gift and because you are unique you should treasure the gift that has been given to you. Don't look at what others are doing – I know it's difficult – just focus on what your passion is and believe that opportunities will open up that will allow you to share that passion.

When I walked into Capital Radio in the mid-80s, my intention was to stay there for just 12 months to save enough money to go to teacher training college, as I was adamant that I was called to be a schoolteacher. 24 months after I first walked through the doors of Euston Tower (the home of Capital Radio at the time), I realised that I was still there and the plan to become a teacher had gone out of the window. The reality is, the plan was being fulfilled, I just didn't realise it at the time. I performed one voiceover imitating a film character and before I knew it I was being paid to share my voice and so the radio career began. That was 25 years ago and during that time I have worked at many radio stations covering all genres of music and talk radio too!!

I share this with you as you may be in a place as you read this foreword of not knowing exactly what it is you want to do. Maybe you're struggling with direction. You may be thinking about just how valuable you are as a female, maybe there are statements that are echoing in your mind from your childhood and you can't shake those statements off and reach your goal.

Well, what a fabulous time to be in the position you are in. There is an amazing amount of knowledge available at your fingertips and this book alone gives you access to the stories of some phenomenal women. You have access to those women and you have access to their experiences.

Remember, life's lessons will need to be re-taken until you learn, so embrace the pages of this book. Embrace the women and their stories and perhaps you might not need to re-take the lessons as many times as some of the writers of these letters.

Time is precious, and these letters for your generation will allow you to utilise the time you have more effectively. Pick up the mantle and ensure the generation that follows you does the same.

Embrace, enjoy and take on your own and the next generation.

With Love

Angie Greaves

TRICIA BAILEY

DEAR YOUNG WOMAN

My name is Tricia Jenise Bailey and I am proud to introduce myself as the co-director of a graphic design company called Kairos Design Solutions. Kairos Design Solutions was conceived many years before it was actually birthed. It took a while to birth because I spent years saying 'one day I will start a business,' 'when I have the time or the money,' 'after I get my first house . . .' and so the excuses kept coming.

Experience in life has taught me that the things we are afraid of doing can end up being the things we love doing the most.

Just a bit about me . . . I remember having an eventful life as a child. Being the 7th of 8 children and the youngest girl I was never short of love, jokes, ridicule or drama. My family was somewhat musical – all of my siblings either sang or played a musical instrument. It was assumed that I would have a career in the music industry, and even though I have been privileged to rub shoulders with the rich and famous, I always knew that there was yet another purpose for my existence.

My parents were strict disciplinarians. I did not appreciate being disciplined as a young child. I thought my parents were from another planet, but now I fully understand that it was me who was the alien. I was a dreamer as a young girl with a wild and vivid imagination. I still am. Many nights I would dream that I was a multi-millionaire and a business owner with all the money in the world to help those who were less fortunate than myself. I say why stop dreaming when you wake up?

I always pay particular attention to quotes and sayings. My parents had lots of quirky sayings, which I still live my life by. But there is a particular quote that, as a youth, I heard people say (until it actually got on my nerves) and that is '. . . you'll regret it when you're older!' I have lived long enough to know that this quote is true. I left school with above average grades, nothing for me or my parents to be disappointed about, but I have regrets about not pushing myself to do better and to further my education. I regret not starting my business earlier and allowing fear to prevent me. I regret not preparing for the realisation of my dreams. I regret not spending time getting to know the graphic design industry inside and out, including aspects I may not be familiar with or may not even like, including marketing, accounting and more. Had I done this I am confident that my dream of being a millionaire would have already been realised. I now understand that my greatest assignment in my youth was preparation!

Preparation would have allowed me to identify the superficial. Superficial meaning existing or occurring on the surface or appearing to be true or real only until examined more closely. Many times our desires and goals can be this way as we succumb to the pressure of always having to looking nice and attractive and donning the latest fashion. While that has its place it ought not overtake our preparation towards our future.

So young woman, my letter is to advise you to prepare yourself for your future. It is never too early to prepare yourself. Procrastination is the thief of time. Not preparing in your early years will cause that annoying saying to be true '…you'll regret it when you're older!' Preparation can be a long journey, like getting to the top of a mountain, but it's completely obtainable and totally worth the effort. Start climbing the mountain of preparation today, and you'll be well on your way to realising your dreams.

I'll see you at the top!

Tricia Bailey

SINITTA

DEAR YOUNG LADIES

I am stunned into silence and stillness as I write to you; I have so much to pour out, I don't know where to begin!

Growing up as a young Black American girl in the UK was an interesting experience for me. The first thing my boarding school did was to put me into elocution lessons so that I could learn to speak 'properly.' I guessed my American accent was unacceptable. In the school choir I was told to sing quietly because I couldn't sing! I guessed my singing was unacceptable.

My mother had raised me as a vegetarian, but my Head Mistress had never heard of one and dismissed the notion as nonsense. I guessed that maybe I was wrong not to eat meat like everyone else and tried to force pork chops and other things down, only to wind up with allergies and tummy aches!

When I went to Russian Ballet School, no matter how slender I managed to get I still had my African Booty and I was told I would never be a dancer with a body like that. I guessed that no matter what I did I would never lose my butt, so ballet wasn't for me.

I didn't have a father growing up but I had several gay godfathers who loved me so much and I loved them; we are still close now. I guessed that gay men knew how to love and straight men didn't.

When my blind best friend Alistaire wanted to run in the school sports day with me, the teachers laughed at me and then scolded me for being ridiculous and making fun of him. I guessed that blind people shouldn't be expected to do the things that I could do.

When the school cast the parts in the ballet production of Snow White I was told there was no way that I could play Snow White even though I could dance it, because Snow White was beautiful and had skin as white as snow. I guessed that my brown skin was therefore not beautiful.

When I went for a modelling job I thought I was perfect for I was told that at 5ft 4.5 inches I would never be a model. I guessed only tall people could be models.

When I saw a group called Hot Gossip on TV with all white girls and black guys I wanted to be in the group but I guessed that was not going to happen because I didn't fit the concept.

When they were looking for a 'mysterious and beautiful girl' to play the lead in a West End show I guessed that because I was not beautiful I shouldn't even audition.

When I saw black women singing on TV I guessed that I would have to sing soul or jazz or Gospel to be a singer myself.

When Floella Benjamin was the only black female I saw regularly on TV growing up I guessed that only women who were Children's entertainers could be TV stars.

When I started to become successful and do TV interviews and photo shoots, the wrong shade of make up was often applied to my skin so thankfully because I had perfect skin, I would often refuse to have make-up which meant that I didn't look as glamorous as others but at least I looked like me.

Bizarrely after years of elocution lessons my very first job was in The Wiz, a black American musical version of The Wizard of Oz! The choreographer of that show Gillian Gregory (yes the choreographer who choreographed Bugsy Malone) hired me directly from there to perform in a movie called Shock Treatment. Record companies and directors started to swoop all over me and I signed several record deals as a soul singer. When I was asked what kind of music I really wanted to sing I chose Pop! Thames Television signed me to present a Children's TV show called The Wall Game shown in the afternoons on ITV1 for 3 series. The West End opened its arms and I received roles in Cats and the Little Shop of Horrors, Hair, Smokey Joe's Café and my American (natural) accent coming in handy.

Simon Cowell was the only person who understood my vision and gave me a chance as a Pop star not a Soul star. Radio stations agonised over my tracks. They saw a black face and then heard a Pop voice so no one knew what to do with my songs! Music was still segregated on the radio in those days. Finally Simon Cowell took my picture off of the front cover and boom! Pop DJ's started to play my music! Then my mother sent me to audition for that West End show and I got it! Yes the one for the Mysterious and Beautiful girl! Suddenly Radio 1, Capital and all of the others were playing my music exclaiming at how different, new, cool, fun, special, unique, refreshing, individual and yes stunning I was!!

I fell in love with a famous black footballer who didn't want to marry only me . . . he wanted to marry me and also have a white girlfriend. I guessed I wasn't enough for a man to be happy with just me and that white girls were more fun or better than me.

Being a lady will never be out of fashion. Take care of yourself, eat healthily, be hygienic and smile, be grateful for all of your blessings, this will give you a graciousness and make you appealing to others. People want healthy, happy and strong role models, we can all teach and help each other. Don't swear! I don't think there is anything cool or attractive about a woman f'ing and blinding; your grandmother wouldn't like it either.

I know this sounds like it's all about me and my racial issues, but it's not really; it's about a changing world and how things were and how they are now. Now almost every high street has a vegetarian option on its restaurant menus. We have Rihanna and numerous pop stars that are black. American accents and rap are the norm and Alesha Dixon and Mel B are TV Judges! Beyoncé is one of the biggest stars in the world and Lupita graces the covers of numerous fashion magazines. Singers like Jesse J have whopping great Gospel voices that are celebrated and respected worldwide! Kim Kardashian is celebrated for her big butt and black women everywhere are proud of their natural backsides and their rounded fit figures. That footballer apparently told a mutual friend recently that he thinks he made a mistake and should have married me! This is nearly twenty years later!!

I am happily with a man, who is white but that's not what makes him better; it's because

I am enough for him and he also loves my two adopted bi-racial children. My gay family is still prominent in my life but I have had successful straight relationships with men who have loved me and I have loved them.

Nowadays people want the same handbags, cars, clothes and hairstyles, but being different is always considered more stylish. If you are different in a good way people will copy you and that's a compliment. Of course there could still be more change and please God more change is coming, but the message in all of this is that you must NOT be discouraged and give up or listen to anyone or any situation that says you can't or shouldn't be or do something you really believe and know you can do and be. It doesn't matter how loud the voices are telling you 'No '– even the voices inside your own head that make you fear and pull back from trying to do new things. SILENCE them with your actions and by moving forward with your plans.

My blind friend Alistair and I did exactly that, two eight year-olds changed the whole face of our school.

On sports day when it was time for our class to run, we made everyone be quiet and told them no one was allowed to cheer or yell. We asked our teacher Mr Davis to stand at the finish line and yell Alistair's name repeatedly so that Alistair could follow the direction of his voice. When the race started all of our class started to run our very fastest in complete silence except Mr Davis shouting, 'Come on Alistair, you can do it! Run faster, faster! This way come on, you can do it!!' Guess what? I came first and Alistair came second!! See what happens when you silence the naysayers with your actions and you move forward uninterrupted and undisturbed by their doubts and disbelief in you! I can tell you that by the end of that race everyone was rushing to congratulate Alistair and the biggest cheer ever went up when he crossed the finishing line, even the people who lost to him were happy for him!

Whatever the desires of your heart, they were put there by God and put there for a reason. You are doing yourself and God a disservice if you bow down to oppression, fear and do not fulfill your destiny and live the life you are called and born to lead. You will know these things because they will speak to you in a very unique way. A way that makes you feel different and determined, even against the odds. Look out for these hints and hunches and never run away from them. Explore, question and understand them and once you see that they are 100% honest, go for it. You will be surprised how easily they actually happen.

My past probably sounds hard to you, but you know what? Every single thing I wanted actually happened, although not necessarily the exact way I wanted them to.

Listen to these stories, learn from us, it's more than about how hard it used to be, because I know for you it is still hard a lot of the time and I don't want to underestimate or belittle that. We all have our struggles – they just affect us in different ways. Always remember if you are pure in your heart and you are kind to people and value the right things and the right ways you shouldn't go far wrong. Equip yourself with the best chance that you can. Education, training, practice – be the best you that you can be.

I heard once that success is when opportunity and preparation finally meet . . . Be ready!

Lastly, love. Love really is more important than money or anything else but money makes life easier. Money gives you more choices and more freedom. I am not saying become obsessed with money, but work hard and save so that you always have enough or even a bit more than you need so you don't have to sweat too much, especially when you are older.

I love you guys and I hope this helps

Sinitta

JESSICA ELLIOTT

DEAR SUPERSTAR! (YES YOU ARE!)

I hope this letter finds you well?

I am writing to give you a bit of encouragement because let's face it we all need it at times. When things get hard, giving up seems like the only thing to do. Trust me girl, I've been there. But to achieve success you have to push on through and remember how much you want it; and you have to want it real, real bad! Whatever 'it' is: that dream job, the business that everyone else thinks is a stupid idea, that university place; the next few lines that you read will hopefully help you see that although we can not always control what happens to us we are in fact masters of our own destinies in how we choose to deal with situations.

So, I hate to break it to you but even in 2015 (the year I write this letter), although as females we have accomplished so much and have had many equality triumphs, the odds are still stacked against you. You are still likely to get paid less than the boys, you will still find it harder to find a job as a young woman and some of your career choices may seem limited or gender cast but should you ever let these facts stop you? Hell no!

I am a woman, I am black, I am short, I am young and I like to wear 'fashionable' clothes. Even more things that in theory will go against me because of nothing more than people's perceptions. I started my business aged just 20, possibly quite naive to the fact that these things even mattered, which is probably a good thing. I quickly taught myself that you have to believe in yourself or no one else will and I say the same to you Hun! It's so, so true!

Running my business for the past 8 years I have begun to realise that the world of entrepreneurship is very much a man's one! But through realisation I have learned the power of being comfortable with who you are and that being different is your biggest strength. Wouldn't it be boring if we were all the same? Thankfully, I learned that all the things that are different to that of my male counterparts are what consumers, the media and the world at large now crave. So girl, embrace your differences, go rock the world in your heels and show them that girls can do it just as well if not better than the boys. Yes 'statistically' the odds may still be stacked against us girls, but there are so many amazing women rocking the show in business at the moment that more and more the true value of having high powered women in corporate firms or dealing with female business owners is being driven home, and so it should! You are awesome and there are so many other awesome girls out there just like you.

I often get asked how I got started I hope you are reading this as someone who wants to create your own income and have an idea for a business or have already started (if you are the latter then congrats). The truth is you just have to make a start. Even a small start is a start. You don't have to have a lot of money. We are in a time where thanks to the Internet, the world is at our fingertips. From the age of 10, I would sit in my room and plan my dance school in my diary. It is never too early to make a start and help always seems to come to you if you show that you are keen. Don't be scared to ask for help either. People, especially those who you think have already made it or who you admire, are usually only too happy to help you, offer advice or point you in the right direction. But if you don't ask you will never know.

Mistakes and failure are also cool. Yes you are a 'superstar' but even superstars are allowed mistakes. In fact I no longer see mistakes as mistakes, they are just choices we make that don't go our way and we can learn from them. Therefore do not be afraid to share your experiences, you never know, you may stop another girl from making that choice. Likewise listen to the experiences of others. Often what's right or not right for others may not necessarily be the right decision for you, but at least it will give you an alternative viewpoint on things. The most important thing to learn is that in life you will make mistakes; sometimes quite big ones. Don't beat yourself up. Take whatever consequences come with it. Really learn the lesson that will have been taught to you and move on in a positive way. I have made many mistakes and tried projects and businesses that have fallen flat on their face. Although I may not have seen it at the time, looking back those things were all part of my progression. Do not be afraid to fail for if we knew we couldn't fail what would be the point in attempting anything?

Another thing I hate to break to you is that if you are doing well, chances are people (including women) may not like you. I once heard someone say, 'If people are not talking about you, you are not doing well enough.' In the early days what people thought of me really bothered me – almost like I sought validation from people that I didn't even know. Growing up we all want to fit in. I can relate to that but to shine like the true superstar you are you have to show you are totally unique.

Don't let the insecurities of others rub off on you. Stay focused on what you want to achieve and let them talk. You may also lose friendships, as once you become truly focused on a goal your interests may change, which may cause you to grow apart from certain people. But ask yourself, if this happens how much of a friend was that friend in the first place? With growth, new friendships blossom and often with like-minded people, whose eyes are on similar prizes to you, which is great for bouncing around ideas as running a business can get lonely. I'm not suggesting for a minute that you ditch your old friends but just be aware that this can happen. You are not the first and certainly won't be the last and it is SO important that you are only surrounded by positivity, love, commitment and support.

Which leads nicely on to relationships. When it comes to being in a relationship never settle for second best. Always only ever be with someone who will be supportive of your dreams and aspirations and see you for no less than the Queen that I know you are. Never allow a partner to dull your shine or make you do anything that you think will then validate your worth to them. You are totally exclusive and worthy of nothing less than total and utter greatness. Yes, no one is perfect but someone can be perfect for you and if they can't see how truly amazing YOU are then it is their loss. They'll be back when they see how successful and happy you are (again I've been there!).

The next point will probably upset parents around the world so sorry in advance! You are always going to have people in your life who 'think they know best.' The fact is you know yourself better than anyone. We all know that certain cultures often dictate the types of career you must choose but guess what? The only thing you must do is what excites you! Parents may not always know what's best however they do want the best for you! If there is something you are truly passionate about, fight for it. Make your parents see that you are serious about it and it is a valid career choice or vocation for you. Work hard and go for it. Parents often suggest safe careers for you. Ones that they know or even the job that they currently do, but ultimately you have to study the subject, or work in the job so YOU have to be happy with the choice.

It's also ok to not know what you want to do. Although I have an established business I still relish opportunities where I get to do something a bit different from time to time. One thing leads to another and often what you think you want to do isn't what you end up doing. So do what you like at the time and when choosing what subjects to study do what you know you are good at.

I really hope that this letter has helped you to now plod on through to get to the end goal; wherever that may be! The most important thing in life is to be happy! So do that! I wish you a successful and prosperous life, filled with love, happiness and acceptance. Go rock the world Beautiful and allow everyone to see how brightly you can shine!

With lots of love always

J x

Jessica Elliott, founder of J's Dance Factory

RONKE
LAWAL

I am so happy that I am writing you this letter and I am even happier knowing that you will be reading it.

I would like to start this letter by letting you know how truly amazing you are. It doesn't matter that we haven't had a chance to meet (or tweet) yet, but I want you to know that I know that you are amazing and I want you to believe it. I want you to know that anything and everything is possible in life but it's just not always going to be easy. You'll be distracted once in a while, it happens to the best of us. It might be a cute boy with a nice

23

smile, a celebrity's glamorous lifestyle or those never-ending deadlines for schoolwork.

It's OK. We all get distracted by so many things, but don't allow those distractions to make you lose track of who you really are. Don't allow those distractions to make you forget how wonderful you are and how wonderful your life can be, each and every day.

I remember growing up with so many insecurities. 'Am I pretty?' 'Do people like me?' 'Will I be successful?' So many questions and so many doubts. My doubts were my distractions, I couldn't shake them. I grew up on a council estate in Hackney. It wasn't exactly luxurious but the community and my family made it home, yet I still had those fears and doubts about where would I end up. Would I always be on an estate? At school I was a bit of geek, I didn't mind that but there were times when I pushed myself hard because I didn't want to let anyone else down. I wasn't even thinking about myself, I was thinking about my teachers and my parents. Would I be successful? During puberty some of the girls in my school would tease me. They would call me 'ugly' I look back now and know that they were trying to hurt me because sometimes, people are cruel. But I still doubted my own beauty. I still worried about how people would perceive me.

Why am I telling you this? My Dear Wonderful One, when I finally began to stop doubting myself and my ability I was able to see beyond what I feared; I started to realise how great life could be. The key to realising how amazing you are is by trusting yourself. It is by finding out who you are and being proud of every single inch of yourself. I don't mean just being able to take a good selfie, I mean being able to sit by yourself and really like who you are when no-one else is there to distract you, when no one else is there trying to tell you about yourself.

When I stopped allowing my doubts to be my distractions I became an unstoppable force. Seriously if I had my own reality TV show you would record every single episode! LOL! I stayed true to myself by being friendly, kind, funny and genuine. I was good to myself and to others. I knew when to stop following the crowd and I knew when to walk away from any situation that made me feel sad or uncomfortable. I hope that you will stay true to yourself, I hope that you can be bold enough to stand out from the crowd and let the world see how wonderful you are.

So as I write this letter, I urge you to take a moment to really focus on where you want to be, who you really are and where you want to get to in your life. Mum and Dad might have a certain vision for your life but you must remember that it is your life! Respect their guidance and make them proud by making the very best out of your life. Take the time to really believe the words that I've written in this letter, believe that you have everything in your mind and in your heart to do so many great things. You are beautiful, you are unique, you have skills that nobody else has and the world deserves to experience your beauty, your uniqueness and your talents. Do not let your doubts and fears hide you from yourself. Do not let all those distractions make you think that you have to be like anyone else to lead a great life, that you have to copy anyone else or pretend to be someone that you are not. You are enough. You are Amazing. You are Wonderful.

Remember what I said at the start of this letter, it's not always going to be easy. There will be days when you don't know what to do, who you are or where you're trying to get to. On those days, stop and take a moment to appreciate yourself. Listen to your favourite music, eat your favourite food, talk to your favourite friend. Take a moment My Wonderful One, but when that moment has passed read this letter again and remember that you are who I have addressed you to be. You are Wonderful.

With Love

Ronke Lawal

ANNMARIE LEWIS

DEAR QUEEN IN THE MAKING . . .

Do you know that's what you are?

YOU really are!! Has anybody taken the time to tell you how precious and amazing you are? How strong, impressionable, talented, carefully crafted and gorgeous you are? How full you are of potential that's bursting to come?

Well let me first say YOU are free to be YOU. The incredible you! The 'its okay to be me' you! The formidable you! The totally lovable you! The 'it's ok to make a mistake' you! The lonely you! The sad and not so sure you! The confident you! The insecure you! The 'I'm strong' you! The 'I need a little help' you! Ultimately the UNEQUIVOCAL you!

Gosh where to start! There's so much I want to say it's hard to contain it in one letter. I can't write to everybody so I write to the young lady who is like me when I was your age! I write to the lost and broken young woman who is supremely gifted but may not know it. Confident in some areas yet masks the pain inside. Defensive and so hard she lets no one break down those barriers – a self-defence mechanism. I write to the one who was abused and rejected even though she may or may not be living within a safe home. To the one who feels unloved, that she doesn't deserve love, or seeks love in all the wrong places. To the one who has secret dreams and desires, but isn't quite sure she can make it. To the one who has been gossiped about and has gossiped about others with no understanding of the true harm; to the one who has bullied and is being bullied. I write to the one who knows they have everything to live for and the future is bright and I say to the one who feels they have nothing to live for, fast forward 5, 10, 20 years my precious daughter you will see how much you do!

Beautiful one . . . Yes YOU: Truly you are beautiful; fearfully and wonderfully made. One of a kind; your own unique design; carefully thought about and shaped to be an amazing person with a specific purpose to fulfil.

Maybe you've never heard this about YOU before or maybe you have loads of people telling you this. Maybe you think who ME? Or maybe you think YES me! Maybe you've been hurt and scarred so deeply, like I was at 11, that you don't know how to believe or receive this. Maybe you don't know how to love or maybe you are SO loved you know this to be true. Maybe you've already experienced some of life's wonderful things or are already showcasing your gifts and talents. Or maybe you're shy and waiting for someone to recognise them. Maybe you've never known life's wonderful things and are praying someone will rescue you and give you a glimpse.

The journey ahead is so exciting and you're gonna be grown for a long time; so hang on to your youthful days, and enjoy being a young girl or a young woman; you'll be an 'adult woman' soon enough. Slow down, take your time and get out of the fast lane, because sometimes we have a way of getting into situations that we just aren't grown enough to handle!

Now I'm not trying to lecture you, I'm just sharing what I wish someone would have told me. It is ok to slow down, stop for a minute and breathe!

Let me just touch on this issue of love and looking for it in all the wrong places. You're living in a generation of the 'ride or die chick', 'fast men' and 'fast money'. Baby girl, you don't have to do that to yourself. You don't have to find love in men and money; you don't have to hide behind drink and drugs; you really don't. And deep down you know it isn't you. You don't have to be tied up with self-hate and self-harm, literally dying to fit in; to belong. Go on and dare to be different.

When I finally learned to love myself, it changed my whole life and it was a love like none other (well except for the indescribable love I found when I gave my life to Jesus at 30) but that's a different story! You may ask 'Well Annmarie how did you do that?' Well Daughter I'm glad you asked! Listen . . . Wherever you're at now and no matter what you may be facing, there's something so very precious deep down inside of you that nothing and no one can take away from you. The most precious thing I ever discovered about myself was my PURPOSE, my PASSION and my PAIN!

Learning about these three things has enabled me to go from the pit to the palace, literally! From facing homelessness – living a semi-road life, to being a regular visitor at Buckingham Palace! From no hope to all hope; from believing I was unlovable and that I didn't deserve to be loved to experiencing unimaginable love; that I was unclean because a close family friend abused me, from feeling I deserved less than because the doctors said I couldn't have children, to being a spiritual mother, supporter and counsellor to hundreds over the years! What a transformation! Yes I praise God for the turnaround! When I discovered that being a mother didn't mean I had to give birth to my own natural children, that indeed I have mothered the motherless and been a mother spiritually and emotionally to so many throughout my life . . . it was the most humbling, precious, rewarding and incredible blessing I have experienced. That being abused didn't mean I could no longer be loved. That the feeling of being rejected, abandoned and alone didn't mean I wasn't deserving of love, neither that I wouldn't ever trust anyone again; that being a dark skinned girl, in a predominantly light skinned family didn't mean I was less than or wasn't as good and vice versa. When I discovered my God-given, God-driven purpose and passion for working with young people – some just like me, some nothing like me – I discovered such a depth of compassion for people from all walks of life; I developed an unstoppable determination that remains to this day and went to loving ME beyond measure!

This journey has helped me to unlock and understand the pain of some areas in my past. I say some because I also had an incredibly brilliant and beautiful childhood in a very loving home. Discovering my passion and purpose gave me the insatiable desire to strive for excellence. I soon realised that if I wanted to grab hold of the love of my present, and the joy of my future, I had to address and let go of the pain of my past. I learned to stop pressing the self-destruct button and to start to reconstruct me!

A big breakthrough was when I learned to stop making permanent decisions based on temporary feelings. I cannot reiterate that sentence enough. Don't make a decision that could affect the rest of your life, based on the way you feel now. I wish I could have known twenty years ago, what I do now. However, this is the next best thing because I can share with you what I would have loved someone to share with me growing up. That you do get through it, you do come out so blessed and life can be such a joy; that perhaps some of the negative things you're experiencing now won't be that way forever.

Queen of the future (That's right you're a princess now) I encourage you never to view your blackness, no matter how that is made up, as anything other than great! Every warm and wonderful shade encompasses your strength and your beauty.

Your ancestors were people of great strength, imposing character and passions! Slavery is a significant part of history but it is not ALL of your history, neither is all your ancestry and slave mentality your legacy! I dare you to explore your true culture and discover a journey of amazement you may never have been told about.

The black presence in Britain dates back years so just to start you off:

- LADY SARA FORBES BONETTA (1843 - 1880) was rescued from slavery by Captain Frederick E. Forbes of the Royal Navy. He convinced King Ghezo of Dahomey to give her to Queen Victoria of England as a present. She was so loved by the Queen that she was raised as her goddaughter in the British Middle Class.

- MARY SEACOLE (1805 - 1881) was a famous Crimean war nurse who housed wounded soldiers.

- UNA MARSON (1905 - 1965) was a Jamaican feminist, activist and writer. She came to London during World War 2 and was the first black female broadcaster and producer for the BBC.

- MARGARET BUSBY OBE is the first black female publisher who co-founded Allison and Busby Ltd in 1967.

- DIANE ABBOTT MP is the first black female Member of Parliament elected to the House of Commons in 1987.

- MAGGIE ADERIN-POCOCK MBE is an English space scientist and since 2014 she has co-presented the long running astronomy TV programme The Sky at Night.

- MISS DYNAMITE is an English Hip hop and R&B recording artist, recipient of the Mercury Music Prize, two Brit Awards and three MOBO Awards.

In the 21st Century we have lots of stars, from sports to entertainment, presenters, musicians, for example there's DENISE LEWIS OBE – Gold medallist and Heptathlon Olympic athlete, ALESHA DIXON – television judge on Britain's got Talent, actresses WUNMI MOSAKU – Philomena, NATHALIE EMMANUEL – Fast & Furious 7 and NAOMIE HARRIS – Skyfall; SARAH JANE CRAWFORD – BBC Radio 1xtra DJ and presenter for The Xtra Factor; BEVERLEY KNIGHT MBE – three MOBO awards and a lifetime achievement award in music, and an award-winning musical theatre actress.

Then there's little old me from Lewisham. I was the first black female prison officer at Feltham Young Offenders Institute and Remand Centre in 1998; I have a Bachelor of Arts degree in Criminal Justice Specialist, a Masters degree in Applied Anthropology, Youth and Community work; a second Masters degree in Research and I am currently a PhD student in Anthropology, Youth, Crime and Entrepreneurship. Spanning a 20-year career in youth justice, I now run my own social enterprise – Rainmakers Worldwide. I also run a second business which is a leadership and change management consultancy organisation and I'm about to launch a young adult movement. All this and I'm only 38!

The only thing that can stop you in this life is YOU. Don't allow anyone to bind you with their negativity or limit you with their lack of creativity. The sky is not the limit and you don't have to think outside the box – who said there was a box to think outside of in the first place? Life can be limitless if you choose it to be! Live life to the full and throw your all at it – you will surely get a vested return!

Do you know the journey of the pearl? The pearl is one of the most precious and highly valued gems in this world! Natural pearls are rare and valued at hundreds of thousands of pounds. It is said that a merchant man seeking goodly pearls, who when he found one pearl of great price, went and sold all he had and bought it. That is how precious pearls are considered to be, and that is how I want you to consider yourself from this day: A Natural Pearl!

Natural pearls are the rarest kind and they are formed inside oysters. When an oyster gets an irritant inside it, in order to stop that irritant from being a nuisance it produces a secretion and every time it feels this irritation it produces another layer. It continues this process over a three-year period. During this time the layers merge together into one solid circular object that is the pearl. Can you imagine one of the most rare and valued, highly priced gems in the world is formed through irritation!

Think about that when you think about all the irritating things inside you; the irritations you might think about yourself. All the things you want to change, or the things that others say are irritating about you. Or that thing that won't stop bothering you or prodding you inside. That dream, that ambition, that annoying passion that every now and then pokes, prods and just irritates you! It was the external irritation that got on the inside of the oyster that formed this beautiful gem. Imagine the same irritations you think about yourself, that have gotten on the inside of you, by the same token this can become your most prized possession too!

No matter how much or how little has yet been seen by you, from you or of you, I promise you there is so much more to come! Take it from one who knows, has experienced the 'more' and is living my dream right now!

Much Love

Annmarie

LEAH CHARLES-KING

DEAR FRIEND

DEAR FRIEND

I've wanted to write this letter to you for so long. It's not that I didn't want to write it, but more 'where do I begin?' It only seems like yesterday when I was on the same path as you. Big dreams. Broad ambition. The world at my feet. Somehow over the years, life can have a habit of wearing you down.

I'm telling you this now in the hope that you may remember these words in 10 years' time, so that you can share them with the next generation of beautiful, ambitious, powerful and gracious women to come. Reflecting on my own life, I hope the following words will resonate and inspire you for greatness. To the younger me.

The younger you. The dreamer. Don't get crushed by life. Try with everything you've got. Take every opportunity that comes your way; if they don't, make them! Be in control of your own destiny! Invest in yourself! Become multi-skilled and multi-faceted so that no one can deny your talent. Don't burn bridges. Be open. Be honest. Be reliable. Be a go-getter. Go above and beyond. And DON'T QUIT! All those years of being bullied, from school to school, and even at my dream job. It would've been so easy to quit, yet even when my spirit was crushed with tears in my eyes I still stood in the storm. Don't let life's adversities stop you from helping others. Goodness will come back to you, I promise. 'Service to others is the rent you pay for your space on Earth,' said the great Martin Luther King Jr. Be free. Don't be afraid to Love! Even when others hurt you don't let it change who you are. Don't live in fear. Live! You never know what tomorrow may bring. Sometimes you may feel as if you're travelling without moving . . . Desperately working towards your goal without seeing the results you hope for; but don't you dare give up! It's at the moment you quit which may be your breakthrough. Nothing is by accident. Every thing we go through is learning . . . Developing. You may not see it right now but some day you will at the right moment. I'm really proud of you. You've come so far already. I feel your dreams. They're tangible. Now make them happen! So to whoever is reading this, have you ever heard the saying 'Pressure builds diamonds'? Well it does, and you're simply a diamond in the rough! Use my story as motivation.

Go get 'em, Girl!

Leah x

CLAUDINE REID

I want you to believe in yourself and stop those self-sabotaging thoughts, sometimes hard things happen in life and you have to learn to bounce back from every set back. Every day that you wake up you are given the opportunity to do something great. To be the best you can be, to think bigger than you did the day before and to believe in yourself. Today I want you to resolve that you will not quit.

I am sure that by now you realise that life can be similar to a team sport. Every team sport has a strategy. Every player on that team has a role. Every team has a goal or a prize to win.

Take into consideration every team as an opponent, whose aim is to not allow you to win. Your role and skill is to discern who is on your team, who has your back and can help you along the way and who is a distraction.

Life does not always happen in a straight line. Things don't always work out in a logical sequence. Part of your skill is to learn how to navigate the roller coaster of life, and at the same time develop your emotional resilience, your mental capacity, your intellectual capabilities and your spiritual strength. In order to advance I recommend that you tackle one thing at a time.

Your goal must be big enough to get you out of bed in morning, even on those days when you don't feel like it. I had the opportunity to interview Jeff Letz – one of the Founder's of Genistar – who said you should have a B.H.A.G (Big Hairy Audacious Goal.) The future that you are planning for should excite you. Your success should be intentional. All of the successful people that I know planned for their gradual progress. Think about the fastest man in the world, winner of the 100 metres in the Olympic Games in Beijing in 2008 and London in 2012 – Usain Bolt. He planned for his success, he did not just stumble across the finish line. He set his sights on a goal and worked consistently towards his dream. He had to be meticulous about his sleeping habits, eating habits and even his recreational habits. The same principle can be applied to any area of your life. What grades do you want in your exams? What university do you want to attend? Where would you like to live? What type of house do you want to live in? Do you want to start a business? What type of job would you like to have?

There are 7 key points that I want you to grasp and think about on a regular basis. The point of this is to help you to get ahead and not to make the silly mistakes that I made and, most importantly, not to allow negativity to sabotage your progress.

CREATE YOUR CIRCLE OF INFLUENCE

One of the most influential people in my life always says, 'If you hang with turkeys you will be dead by Christmas or Thanksgiving if you live in America'. This simply means understand who you spend your time with. In the end whatever 'they' do, you will end up doing. Who is influencing your actions and habits? Turkeys do not get very far. Even in the month of January they still only have 11 months. Create a circle of people that have a positive influence on your life who will influence you to be the best you can be.

GIVE A SHORT-TERM SACRIFICE

There are times in life when you have to give up something in order to progress to the next level of your greatness. It does not have to be forever it may be for a few months, but I guarantee that you will feel so much better. I have found in life that the things that I have had to work for, or the thing that I sacrificed for, often means so much more to me. Sometimes that short-term sacrifice could be turning off the TV for an extra hour and doing more homework, or giving up that bar of chocolate in order to have a more positive impact on your health, or staying off social media for an extra hour to focus on your studies. Remember this commitment is for you. You are the main person that will reap the benefits.

MAKE YOURSELF ACCOUNTABLE

Have at least 3 or 4 people in your life that you trust and can be answerable to. That means you give them the right to question you. I have found that I needed people in my life like this because I didn't want to let them down, or more importantly I didn't want to let myself down. Allow them to ask you questions about your education, your career goals, your male and female friends, your commitments, your studies and education. The people that you choose should be older than you, and individuals who you respect, trust and have a genuine interest in your well-being.

REQUIRE DAILY EXCELLENCE

Set a standard for yourself and don't compromise. Sometimes it is hard to walk away. But it is important for you to set a standard and maintain it. You must be in a position where you know yourself and your goals and don't settle for anything less than your best. That means you will need to learn to manage your time more effectively. Under the clock we are all equal. Every one has 24 hours in their day. It is what you decide to do with your 24 hours that will make the difference.

MASTER THE ART OF LETTING GO

Some people are not your friends. Just because he said you have nice eyes, that's not a good enough reason to hold on to a toxic relationship. The same can be said for some of your female friends. Some of them are witches with a 'b' and really do not mean you anything good. Let them go! This may cause you to feel that your world is caving in, but I promise you, life will go on and in most cases life will be better without toxic relationships.

SERVE OTHERS

Whilst I was growing up there were some challenging times that I had to learn to navigate my way through. I found that when I made an extra special effort to serve others I felt motivated and empowered. Volunteer, especially for those that are less fortunate than yourself. Work in a nursing home, volunteer at your church, a local youth group or another reputable organisation. It will help you to see life differently as well appreciate what you already have.

WORK HARD TO DEVELOP YOUR CONFIDENCE

Confidence is key. You will find this out in a few years' time, but for now I'd advise you to work on it. Confidence comes with competence. Work hard to develop your talents and skills and when you are good at what you do, you will feel confident about doing it. You will stand out from the crowd.

One of the reasons I wanted to share these lessons with you is because I wish someone had shared them with me. I am sharing this with you now thinking how much different my life would have been if I had let go of certain friends sooner, or if I worked harder whilst I was at school or if I focused on what my teachers instructed and was less concerned about what my friends thought. I remember my light bulb moment when I realised 'this is my life' and I decided to step into who I wanted to be.

You may think it is too late, but let me take this opportunity to assure you it is never too late.

Your Mentor

Claudine

ANGIE
LE MAR

DEAR YOUNGER GENERATION,

I feel honoured to share my thoughts and experiences with you. My life so far has been amazing but I never believed that most of my dreams would have come true.

I was a little girl who loved making people laugh, but I didn't know that I could make a career out of it. I just knew I loved the sound of people laughing because of me. You get to realise later, that we all have our gifts and that was mine.

It's only as I stand here today, looking back at my life, that I can truly understand how I got here. Every step of the way seemed so planned, but it wasn't. It was a journey filled with ups and downs, heartache and disappointments too, but there were a few things that kept me going; and that was the belief in myself and the fact that no one could stop me, even if they didn't get me or understand where I was going, and boy was I going!

One of my teachers told me that I was not going to amount to much. I looked at her and thought, 'How dare you?' I never once believed her. In fact, I thought, 'What a fool she does not know me, I'll show her!'

I spent most of my young years being chucked out of my classes, being labelled as disruptive, the class clown and the lists goes on. It didn't really bother me because I knew deep down I was going to be somebody. When I left school I found out I was dyslexic, which explained a lot of my behavior at school. So I wasn't bad, I just had a few 'issues'.

You may be going through difficult times at school or at home. You may feel like no one understands you, well, you are not alone. I have felt those feelings. I have sat on my bed, thinking, 'Why can't I be like everyone else?' I never felt clever at school, I felt stupid, I felt very odd, and as much as I had a lot of friends, I liked my own company. To this day, I need to have my own space.

Looking back at my life, I truly understand how and why I am here today, I made choices early on in my life that have made me who I am today.

I look at today's society and I know there is a great deal of pressure on you to be educated, to achieve, to be a success, which can be very frustrating because these are the years when you want to have fun.

My parents did not allow me to have too much fun; I was raised in the Church, and had very strict parents. I couldn't go out as much as I would have liked to, but the one activity that I was permitted to go to was drama club, and that was all I needed, my confidence soared. I had found a place where I wasn't judged, I was applauded for the skills and efforts of my natural talent, and it was the perfect environment for me.

I would encourage you to find something that makes your heart sing, that thing that encourages your voice, your heart, and when you discover it you'll find you'll never stop doing it. Not everyone finds their passion at a young age, so don't be discouraged. One day you will find yourself doing something and it will make you feel excited and you'll want to do it again and before you know it, you can't stop doing it. It could be anything, writing, dancing, teaching, sports, whatever it is, you will know.

There are things I do regret. I regret not paying attention in school – although I know why I wasn't interested. But the value of education started to haunt me as I got older and I have had to catch up over the years. Whatever you do in life, value your education, it's not even up for discussion.

I remember when I was younger; sitting in on some deep conversations and sometimes I didn't have a clue about what was being discussed. I had to go away and fix that; you don't want to be left out of any conversations. You don't want people talking around you, over your head because after a while it's not cool. At times it starts to feel embarrassing, you feel inferior, not because you are, but because you are not as well-read as you should be and it does affect you. You lose confidence because you're not up to speed on the topics being raised. I got there in the end through reading a lot, but for me, if there was one thing I could turn back time for, it would be education.

They say if you want to hide something from our community, put it in a book, and here you are reading a great book. I love reading, it's reading aloud that I am not great at. However, I get it, some people can run fast, I can't. That's what I want you to get, that you are the best person to do you. The day you step out of your gift, you are in someone else's dream. I found reading was a way to escape. The information never ends. It's a great habit to have. If you're not a reader, you are missing out on so much, you are just being told through the opinions of others, as opposed to finding out for yourself.

Whenever I hear people say, 'I've never read a book in my life', I am silenced, as I do not know how that is possible, that is actually not something to be proud of.

As I watch the growth of social media from Facebook to Instagram and Twitter, I see more and more young people using this to express themselves, which is great. My only advice would be, watch what you put out on there. Be mindful, as this is fast becoming a place where every feeling is expressed. From simple thoughts, to sexy pictures, to gossip, all of which will follow you into all areas of your life. At times you may see the pictures that feel really expressive at that moment, but as you grow older you will want to delete those images, you will want to forget those statuses. However, the Internet is not so forgiving. Social media companies can hold on to your shared-self forever, so only give away what you can afford to lose. Please don't take what people present on these sites as gospel. If you don't feel confident about who you are or where you are in life, it can be easy to negatively compare. Someone else's life may always look better than yours and this can bring up insecurities. It can make you think that maybe you are being left behind, like you are in some sort of competition or that time is against you.

The same thing you are going for, someone else has just got, and now you feel it's not worth going for. This is a dangerous mindset.

My Mother used to say to me, 'What is for you can not be un-for you.' It took me a long while to understand, but years later, I totally understand that everyone has theirs, and we all get ours at different times. The power is to be happy for those who get theirs before you, because with hard work and determination, you will get yours.

Finding what you love to do at an early age is possible, the passion will not leave you. With or without the rewards you'll want to fulfill your dream, all you have to do is build it with passion and integrity and you will get there, some things you cannot put a price on.

If you have had a difficult start in life, it doesn't have to stay that way or end in difficulty. You can change your mind at any given time. The power of thought and the desire to change, build, and create something amazing is not only possible, but it has been done. I believe that to achieve against the odds is such a powerful gift. You may doubt yourself – especially if you are doing something for the first time – you will come against obstacles, you will find people unsupportive, and that could be family and friends too, but once you are determined and believe in yourself, it will take a lot to stop you.

This is why it's important to share your ideas with only a few, and pick your team wisely. This team is made up of people like you; people who believe in you and encourage you often, they don't ask why, they ask when? When I was growing up my parents used to say, 'Show me your friends and I'll show you who you are.' That speaks volumes now, for more than one reason. If your friends are not going the same way you're going, then you are going the way they are going, and that is all. If they are not going the right way, change your friends, and keep your focus.

Now growing up is not going to be easy, there are going to be difficult patches, and that's life. It's what you do when you are not having a great time, when you feel let down, when everything seems to be failing. In those bad times, please remember this: this too shall pass. Cast your mind back to a really difficult and sad time, that passed, right?

You need all your experiences, you need a gauge for good and bad, it makes you appreciate everything. Some of my tough lessons were learned from trial and error, but it made me tough. Even my dark times, and there have been a few when I didn't feel pretty, I didn't feel funny, I felt over-looked, but as time went by I turned what seemed like a disadvantage to my advantage.

I struggled with auditions as a young actress, so I wrote my own plays. I wanted to make people laugh, even when I was told that black women do not do comedy, I became Britain's first black stand-up comedienne. When I didn't have money to get a director to direct my plays, I directed them myself. My point is I then found that I liked writing and directing, so I went on to train and do courses, because I had found something I wanted to learn more about. This is why I say, in those moments when it looks impossible, look at it again and it will be staring you right in the face, the big 'why don't you do that?' This is what you call successful thinking; this is what will separate you from those who give up.

My last thought is, appreciate life. Life is wonderful; it's full of promises. In this life, throw yourself at everything; be busy and excited to learn something new. Plan your life to be a life that travels, try to learn and experience different people. Learn and respect the cultures of other people. There is so much value in this, get to know how other people live in the world, and don't accept everything that the media gives you, it will change your outlook on the world.

I'm a firm believer in the saying 'whatever you sow you'll reap,' and over the years I have witnessed this. Be a person that sows beautiful kind seeds. I'm not being airy-fairy, this is true. When you think positively and reflect that, it will follow you. Have you ever wondered why some people are miserable and always unhappy? Well, quite a few people wake up to be miserable or angry and as such, so are their lives. Their outlook is bleak, because that's what they attract. So understand that whatever you put out there will come back at some time in your life, so be kind, watch the way you treat people, as you do not know the impact you will have on them, no matter how small.

My brother once told me, 'What the mind can conceive, the man can achieve.' There is nothing too big for your thoughts and dreams. I have done more than I hoped for and now I know it's all possible, I keep believing for bigger.

Look after yourself, take up a sport and if you're a girl reading this, I suggest you take up self-defense, this will build your physical confidence and follow you into everything, also people will rarely mess with you.

I'm hoping my few words have shown you that in my life I made my dreams possible and you are no different, so go and have a great life!

Angie Le Mar x

BIANCA MILLER

Congratulations on being a part of the next generation of female leaders, because I do not doubt that is who you are destined to be. Maintain this thought as you go throughout life, you are a leader – it doesn't matter what you choose to lead in, just make sure you do a good job.

What is a female leader? It is every strong female figure you have around you that you look up to, listen to and adore. It's your mother, sister, auntie, cousin, grandmother, teacher, preacher, businesswoman or maybe even celebrity. If they inspire you to be great, to lead from the front and to stand up and be counted then they are the leader you want to aspire to be.

Don't be afraid to lead, the leaders and the revolutionaries are not always the loud and vivacious ones. Often they are the ones who maintain the spirit of hard work and are conscious contributors. As the saying goes 'A wise (wo)man speaks because (s)he has something to say, A fool speaks because they have to say something.'

Be a woman of value, of substance and of use, who is not afraid to be more than she or her peers ever thought she would.

Understand your strengths and your weaknesses; knowing where you are weak is strength in itself, as you can work towards being better.

Know who you are and the image you want to portray to the world, a good salesperson sells a product with ease, as they know its uses, benefits and the value it adds. In the same way you should know your ability, your advantages and your worth in order to define your 'personal brand' and market yourself for a better future.

Experiment with things you haven't done, not what you always do – it is easy in life to become complacent but it is the innovators who thrive. Life is an ever-evolving process, every day, hour and year you will learn new things that enhance you and your brand. Accept the challenges that bring you closer to your dreams and the ones that simply enhance your experiences. The best way to know if you like or dislike something is to try it.

Do not be afraid to try something new. As Mr Miagi from The Karate Kid once said, 'Daniel son, it is ok to be afraid but must not loose through fear.' We are all afraid, we all have concerns but what separates the good from the great is the ability to overcome those fears. There is no shame in failure, it is better to have tried and failed, than never to have tried at all!

Recognise social media as a platform to exhibit your greatness and not just to socialise. Advances in technology have given you a phenomenal platform to have a voice and global reach, use it with the care it deserves.

Listen more than you speak – You may feel that the older generation do not know what it is like to live nowadays, mum might not understand what a hashtag is or why you would rather send a voice note on WhatsApp than call your friend, but their knowledge and experience holds great value and will shape your thinking. Being a great leader involves having the patience and humility to listen to and learn from others. Imagine navigating the transport system without a map, you would make a number of unnecessary mistakes before getting to your destination. A great teacher or mentor will get you to your destination much faster.

Celebrate your success – there will be times in life when you are perceived as a success, maybe even an 'overnight success' because they didn't see the long hours, sleepless nights and hard work that led you to where you are today. Do not let that stop you from taking a moment to appreciate and celebrate the success you have had. Too often people look for the next piece of work to be done to stay on the treadmill. It is not self-indulgent to celebrate or be proud of what you have done, absorb the moment and use that to motivate you to celebrate the next.

Finally and most importantly, recognise the beauty in you. Do not let any man, woman or child tell you differently. You are beautiful because you are unique and it is your individuality, spirit and ambition that will drive you to be greater than you ever imagined.

As Oscar Wilde said, 'Be yourself, everyone else is taken,' and that's ok because it is you that we want.

My mantra – Be You, Only Better! See you at the top.

With Love

Bianca Miller

DIAHANNE RHINEY

DEAR YOUNG WOMAN

I actually wish I could see you. As I write this letter, I wish I had the time to sit with you and talk with you. To hear your voice. Since I cannot do any of those things, I am writing my heart to you in a letter. I'm praying that these words do not seem useless or boring to you, but rather that in the times when you need them, they are tucked away and read when life becomes challenging or hard.

As a young, beautiful girl, you are probably experiencing a period of your life where you are seeing so much change happen. Our society is constantly changing; how we communicate is changing and our friends may seem to come and go. All of these things can sometimes make us feel unsure of ourselves and who we actually are. Our culture and what you see on TV and social media bombards us with so many messages about how you should look, what you should wear, even how to speak. Sometimes, the things we see online or in the news are unkind or so cruel, they make us question our own identity. I would love to say, that things will change as you get older, but the reality is TV, fashion, music and all the other things that are fighting for your attention will always be there. You simply need to work out the good from the bad so that you can journey through life and have the best success. I want to say some things especially to you that will help you understand your own identity and who you are. Words to encourage you through struggles and any insecurity, because when you understand who you are, you will know your true value, beauty and worth.

YOU ARE BEAUTIFUL, SPECIAL AND LOVED
The first thing I'd like to say to you is this: there is so much that you are becoming. You

are becoming a teenager, a young woman and you are on an exciting, incredible journey. You were created unique; there is no one else out there like you. If you haven't started already, you are on a journey where you will discover your identity. This is an exciting time of self-discovery that at times may seem confusing and scary. In fact, it's a great time to find out about your unique gifts, so start asking all those questions you wanted to ask.

Find a mentor or role model that you can confide in and share what you're thinking. This could be a parent, a teacher or someone you really admire. It's important that you have someone that you can be yourself with, someone who you can confide in, someone who won't laugh at your ideas. Your friends are great, but it's also great to have that special 'go to' person, who you can go to when you need them.

YOUR LIFE REALLY IS AN OCEAN

What on earth does that mean? It means, don't limit yourself to what you see around you. There is a big world out there that is just waiting for you to discover it. I would encourage you to get yourself a map of the world and mark all the places on it that you would like to visit. Travel is one of the best ways for you to get an education. It will give you the opportunity to learn about different places, people and cultures and will also make you appreciate how well-off you are. Have you ever thought about working in an animal sanctuary somewhere in Africa or volunteering to help with not so well-off children in a school in Peru? These are example of experiences that will really help you to grow as a person and you'll probably be surprised at how much you will learn about yourself.

READ, READ AND READ SOME MORE

Whether you pick up an actual book or an e-reader such as a Kindle, I would like to encourage you to read. Just like travelling, reading will get your imagination thinking all sorts of exciting things that are possible. I would suggest you also read about people you like and admire, especially people that have changed history and made the world better for us to live. Reading about women such as Rosa Parks or Madame C. J Walker is a great place to start. Their inspiring stories will teach you that great things really are possible to achieve with hard work.

YOUR WORDS DO MATTER

Just as I am choosing my words today to encourage, it's important for you to know that words can also bring harm. You may have had people talking about you behind your back, or saying things about you that were not true. Perhaps you've been in situations where you have been saying things about other people. I would like to say to you that your words really do matter. Try speaking kind words to your friends and when they are not around, resist the urge to get involved in gossip, no matter how juicy or tempting. A famous writer called Maya Angelou once said, 'People may never remember what you said, but they will always remember how you made them feel.' Just as I hope my words are making you feel valued and loved, try to make your words do the same to others.

VALUE YOURSELF & FIGHT FOR IT

You may have been through so much already, difficulties at school or home. You may feel as though you are not good at anything. When I was a teenager, sometimes I felt unattractive, spotty and unlovable. So in writing this to you, I want you to know that you are clever, funny, sweet, attractive, and lovely. You may not realise it or believe it now, but you are. It may take you many years to 'find' yourself, to believe in yourself and have courage and confidence in yourself. You will take many knocks along the way before you even fully understand some of the things I've written to you. Please, please understand this – don't let anyone tell you that you can't, because you can. Don't let anyone tell you that you are stupid, because you are not. Don't let anyone take advantage of you, because you are worth so much more. With respect, learn to say 'NO' and assert yourself. Try not to be led or forced into doing things that make you feel uncomfortable. Don't ever feel that you have to go along with the crowd just to fit in.

Be confident to stand out, because you do. Don't worry if things get a little tricky because all the challenges will make you stronger. And even if you fail at something, never ever be afraid to try again. If you believe in something and want it badly, it is worth fighting for.

ENJOY THE JOURNEY

Above all, I'd like to tell you to be yourself and enjoy the journey. Never be afraid to be you, even if it means being different. Embrace life and what it has to offer and don't be afraid to take a chance. Get good advice from your mentor or 'go to' person and believe in yourself. Life's journey will have many ups and downs; so don't be too hard on yourself. You will meet many new people along the way, so choose your friends wisely, and remember these kind words.

Finally, you have so much to offer this world, you are probably not even aware of just how brightly you shine. Soon, you will see it in yourself and then you'll realise how much of a beautiful gift you are. So enjoy your life. Live, laugh, dance and be happy. Learn to love yourself first and then you'll be able to love others and be loved.

From – The girl who has been in your shoes and knows it is possible to fly

Diahanne

SAMANTHA GOLDING

DEAR FRIEND,

When I was 11 years old, I couldn't wait to be a teenager. When I was a teenager, I couldn't wait to be 21. I remember clearly, on my 21st birthday a close friend said to me 'that's it now ... the years are going to fly by ...' I looked at her in total bewilderment and after a few seconds, to make myself feel better, I concluded that she was only saying this to me because she was upset that she was fast approaching her 30's!

When I reached the milestone of 30 years old, I was very happy with my life. I was in the 6th year of a great marriage, owned a couple of properties and enjoyed my job. But even then, a small part of me wished that I could rewind a few years and change some things in my 20's. Now that I've reached 40, I marvel at my achievements. I've had a total career change and I'm on track to achieving some life changing personal goals. You can't beat that feeling, but even then, a part of me still wishes that I could re-write some poignant moments in my 30's.

I guess my friend was right – time has literally flown by, or so it seems. Nearly 19 years later it's still a running joke between us, but little did I know that such a simple statement would have such a profound effect on my life.

Simply put, TIME IS PRECIOUS, yet like so many things in life, it is often undervalued and unappreciated.

That is why what you do in your youth is so important. I know it probably doesn't seem that way and why should it? Youth is a fantastic thing. It's about having fun, spreading your wings, exploring life and being carefree. Believe me I've had my fair share of fun and I wouldn't want to rob you of that – however, just remember that whatever you do – or dare I say don't do – in your youth, will have an impact on your future. Sounds heavy, I know. But it's not meant to frighten you – honestly! As much as I'd love to be able to rewind time and advise my younger self of what to avoid and the best choices to make – I can't! So instead, I'll take a few moments to share my experience with you so that you have an even better opportunity to become the best teenager, young woman and adult that the world has ever seen.

Someone shared something with me a few years ago and I'd like to pay it forward to you. 'Don't make decisions based on your present . . . make decisions based on your future.' You're probably wondering how on earth that's possible! Well, it is. In a nutshell, don't just think about here and now, think about where you want to be in a few months or a few years' time. The key thing here is to plan ahead. For example, you might not want to do that course now but think about how it could benefit you in the future. I know way too many people who are doing their GCSE's in their 30's and 40's, wishing that they had done them when they were younger. If they had someone to tell them how important their qualifications would be in the future, I dare say they would have buckled down and worked harder. This principle can be applied to so many things. Your savings, your business plan, your health – anything! You're never too young to plan ahead. In fact, the earlier you start, the better. If you're one step ahead you're less prone to stumble upon surprises and you'll go far at an accelerated pace. Don't get me wrong, you can still get far ahead in life by making mistakes and not pre-planning. After all, a large percentage of people do and they'll probably tell you that they achieved their goals by learning from their mistakes. That's all very well, but why take the scenic route when you can get there in half the time? It's less time consuming and less painful to learn from someone else's mistakes instead of constantly making your own. It's all about working smarter and not harder.

I remember growing up at home with four other siblings. As much as it was fun it was also very fierce, particularly as I was the youngest child! I'm sure some of you can identify with this. Having to contend with older brothers and sisters meant that I didn't always get the biggest piece of chicken at dinner time, or the best seat in front of the TV. A lot of the time I was at the back of the queue and being too afraid to fight, I simply accepted that this was the way it was going to be.

Young woman, your positioning is so important. Do not be content with staying at the back of the queue. You are a unique individual and regardless of how great or small, there is always something that you can contribute in order to make a positive difference to society. If you want the best, you will have to push through the crowd of those who seem bigger and better than you and reposition yourself at the FRONT. Having this vantage point will expose you to amazing opportunities. You will see things that others cannot see. You will have access to things before anyone else and more importantly; you will get first choice of the best instead of the leftovers. With integrity and fervency do whatever you can to stay ahead of the game. Don't settle for anything less. You are worth so much more.

Young Woman, I want the absolute best for you. Please don't be afraid to pursue your dreams. If you get it wrong, so what? Simply move on to plan B and try again. Do whatever you can to develop your skills and empower yourself with knowledge. It might mean having to dust off that book; enrol on that course or, dare I say, change your circle of friends (ouch!). If you want the best, you're going to have to surround yourself with the best. Be in the company of confident people who can stretch you, challenge you and have fun with you. Remember, the key thing in all of this is to manage your time and not to waste it – there's so much that you can do NOW that will save you precious time in years to come.

Young Woman, make me proud! I want to read about your success in the newspapers, see your name on the country's Rich List and celebrate you as a leading pioneer in society.

No doubt, in 10 years time when I'm 50, I'll look back and wish that I could change some of the choices that I'm making now. So, do you know what? I'm going to use my time wisely and do the best that I can do NOW to make that 'I wish I'd done . . .' list as small as possible. It would be great if you could join me and do the same.

Wishing you great success

Samantha Golding

JENNI STEELE

My name is Jenni Steele and I am the
National Ambassador for Domestic Violence
UK and a Broadcast Journalist in radio.
Before we get started I wanted to let you
know that the only thing that can stop you
from achieving your dreams is YOU!! There
is limitless potential in us all, as long as YOU
believe in yourself and work hard you can and
will achieve. My legacy that I leave today is
proof of this . . .

As a teenager I found myself in a very
unhealthy situation. At the time I did not
understand what I was involved in because
nobody had spoken to me about healthy and

unhealthy relationships with boys before. I am taking this opportunity to give you some signs of a healthy or unhealthy relationship along with support and key numbers that can assist you should you find yourself or a friend in an unhealthy situation and have nobody to talk to or share your queries and concerns with. I make myself personally available in the strictest of confidence, as I know what it is like to be scared to tell anyone or not feeling comfortable sharing with friends or family. Please understand that it is normal to have fears and be scared. Talking to someone is the first steps towards dealing with any situation.

HEALTHY RELATIONSHIP INSIGHTS

- Respect in a relationship means that each person values who the other is, understands this and would never challenge the other person's boundaries.

- Trust – There's no way you can have a healthy relationship if you don't trust each other.

- Separate identities – in a healthy relationship everyone needs to make compromises. But that doesn't mean you should feel like you're losing out on being yourself. When you started going out, you both had your own lives (families, friends, interests, hobbies, etc.) and that shouldn't change. Neither of you should have to pretend to like something you don't, or give up seeing your friends, or drop out of activities you love. And you also should feel free to keep developing new talents or interests, making new friends, and moving forward.

WARNING SIGNS

When a boyfriend or girlfriend uses verbal insults, mean language, nasty putdowns, gets physical by hitting or slapping, or forces someone into sexual activity, it's a sign of verbal, emotional, or physical abuse.

Ask yourself, does my partner:

- Get angry when I don't drop everything for them?

- Criticize the way I look or dress, and say I'll never be able to find anyone else who would date me?

- Keep me from seeing friends or from talking to other boys?

- Want me to quit an activity, even though I love it?

- Ever raise a hand when angry, like they are about to hit me?

- Try to force me to go further sexually than I want to?

These aren't the only questions that you can ask yourself. If you can think of any way in which your partner is trying to control you, make you feel bad about yourself, isolate you from the rest of your world, or harm you physically or sexually, then it's time to speak to someone who can help support you. Let a friend or family member know what's going on and make sure you're safe.

It can be tempting to make excuses or misinterpret violence, possessiveness, or anger as an expression of love. That's exactly what I did. Even if you know that the person hurting you loves you, it is not healthy. No one deserves to be hit, shoved, or forced into anything he or she doesn't want to do.

On a happier note, relationships can be one of the best and also most challenging parts of your life as you approach womanhood. They can be full of fun, romance, excitement, intense feelings, and occasional heartache too. Whether you're single or in a relationship, remember that it's good to be particular about who you get close to. If you're still waiting, take your time.

Think about the qualities you value in a friendship and see how they match up with a healthy relationship. Work on developing those good qualities in yourself. If you're already part of a couple, make sure the relationship you're in brings out the best in both of you.

At the bottom of this letter you will find contact details from different organisations that provide support to women. All services surrounding unhealthy relationships and domestic violence are strictly confidential, they have specially trained people on the other end of the phone and if you are really worried you do not have to give your personal details to get advice or support. The one thing I ask of you, is that if your friend or family member comes to you in confidence please treat them how you would want to be treated if you were that situation, as the judgement from others was what stopped me and stops many others daily from telling anyone. It kept me silent and I ended up being in a more dangerous position for a longer period of time.

Happy, confident and successful is the woman who speaks to you today. An award-winning inspirational woman who turned a negative relationship experience into a positive situation to support others.

A little secret of mine is reading this very quote below (a favourite of mine) to myself daily.

'I know who I am. I am not perfect.
I'm not the most beautiful woman
in the world. But I'm one of them.'
Mary J. Blige

My contact details will follow in this book if you feel you have nowhere to turn, or need support, strength or motivation at any time. Please feel free to contact me personally I reply to every email personally and support people from all around the globe.

Jenni

CONTACT NUMBERS FOR SUPPORT

24-hour National Domestic Violence
Freephone Helpline for women
0808 2000 247

www.TheHideout.org.uk is a safe website for teenagers and fully confidential.

www.DVUK.org has a directory that can put you or your friends in the direction of services in your local area.

MS.
DYNAMITE

DEAR SISTER!!

I hope this finds you well! I am writing a letter, hopefully entailing some encouragement and support to inspire and remind you of just how amazing you are! You, such a special and important young woman, mean so much to the world. May your heart remember your worth, your mind connect with your knowledge and your power evoke YOUR TRUTH!!

From the moment we are born we are taught to look outside of ourselves for our answers, our identity, our worth, our value, and our beauty. We are all born unique and gifted with the blessing of being the ONLY 'you' on the planet, only to be constantly compared, judged, squashed into league tables, moulded into statistics, then poked, prodded and pinned with labels!! We're discouraged from trusting our intuition and instead, encouraged to be anything and everything but what we naturally are!

Raised in this 'modern' society & culture that persuades, influences and blatantly brain-washes us, we can often experience an entire lifetime being bombarded with stereotypes and a shallow, single minded, idealistic perspective of beauty, which leaves us feeling anxious & stressed, just 'existing,' trying to fit into some-one else's box or walk someone else's path, in someone else's shoes, wishing someone else's wishes & chasing someone else's dreams! We can end up with issues that are not even our own, just because we've taken on someone else's idea of who we should be and what our priori-ties should be!

For instance you might secretly like a differ-ent style or brand of clothes to the ones you wear, but because our personal taste is not popular to that of everyone else, we conform and go against the things that would make us more comfortable inside. This need to 'fit in' or not 'stand out' can transcend into the ideas we have about our physical shape and size, our bone structure, hair texture and even our skin colour or tone. How can we ever know ourselves, or obtain a true sense of happiness if we reject and deny who and what we are, just because it doesn't fit the mould of the masses?

Please don't take this as preachy or judgmental. No matter how much I now understand about the healing and empowerment found in 'self-love', I'm still learning. But what I can tell you is that gifts can be found within the journey no matter how low it may push us and blessings can often be disguised or hidden in the most painful situations. It's about perception & perspective!

So let me just start by telling you that . . . YOU ARE BEAUTIFUL, AMAZING & WONDERFUL JUST THE WAY YOU ARE, INSIDE AND OUT, RIGHT HERE, RIGHT NOW!!!

I know that probably doesn't mean much, because all that ever really matters is what we think and feel about ourselves. But if you do suffer or struggle with these types of insecurities too, then I hope that I can offer you a few ideas that might help you start to see your beauty and YOUR TRUTH!!

Now if someone had talked to me about 'perspective' and 'perception' at 15 when I lived in a hostel, drinking and smoking my life into oblivion, feeling unloved, misunderstood and totally pissed at the world, believing it had completely let me down I would have definitely hurled endless expletives at them! LOL!!

I used to feel how you might do now, like it isn't possible to get over pain. I believed that it was everlasting and that I was always going to hate my life and that I'd hurt the way I did, forever! I thought dwelling and wallowing in it was the only way, but over a decade later, I'm thankful for the challenging trials and tribulations thrown at me. I've grown to understand that without the testing times we wouldn't experience the magic within our stories. The thing is, it really didn't have to take this long, if only I'd understood my power and ability to change my perspective and perceptions. The quick and short of it is that if you'd like to feel and experience better, you can start right now by changing YOUR thinking!

This is not to blame yourself for whatever you may be going through, this is to help you connect with your POWER. Believe me, you have so much more than you realise and you can start to connect with it through taking . . .

RESPONSIBILITY:

Whatever the situation, confrontation, or altercation,
If we want to reach a solution and achieve emancipation,
We can start by looking in the mirror and begin communication,
We become secure by accepting our flaws, empower your foundation,
Because there's not much to gain from shame or from blame,
We merely prevent our healing and simply prolong our pain,
We can cry rivers and remain the victim, but we do this in vain
Our freedom can never come, if it means 'waiting' on other people to change.

Taking responsibility is a matter of looking at where our own decisions may have contributed to our current dilemma. How and with whom do we choose to spend our time? Do we feel good in their presence and do they bring out the best in us? If not, why do we continue to keep their company? How do we think about and speak to ourselves? Do we support ourselves with loving and kind nurturing patience? Or do we constantly doubt and degrade ourselves with even the simplest of negative phrases? Such as 'ah I'm such an idiot' or 'I can't do anything right' or 'I'm not pretty enough or smart enough.' The things that we allow to continue within our lives, including our 'self' talk are our choice. I'm not saying it's easy, but there is definitely no power to be found in blame. No strength or change can come from continuously complaining about our issues with no effort or action attempted to alter them. Power and change can only come once we are willing to be brutally honest and brave with ourselves. Power begins when we are really ready to take those first steps toward change, and in order to do this we must . . .

REFLECT:

For some this could mean simply taking 5 minutes in your day to sit quietly, breathe, be calm, rest your soul and listen to within, but for others this could mean full on, focused, mindful meditation!! Either way it's about hearing, accepting and appreciating your own voice, connecting with YOUR TRUTH!! Replace anything damaging that takes us from our authenticity. Learn to quiet the ever-present ego and silently surrender to the 'self' that we keep secret. We learned to take on concepts that just don't resonate with us, so we can unlearn and only start to truly know ourselves, when we learn to listen to our own voice. Have you ever really taken the time to get to know you? Well now's the time! Get to like, love and LISTEN to 'you' and your inner talk. Find YOUR passions, YOUR desires, YOUR needs and keep listening and practicing being true to YOU! Some people won't like it. You might ruffle a few feathers and even lose a few friends, but this is far less painful than losing yourself! There is great power in the ability and courage to honour our own values, but it will also take a certain amount of . . .

RESPECT:

Face anything and everything you need to, in order to learn respect for YOURSELF!! Once we have self-respect everything will naturally fall into place, like the honesty & assertiveness it takes to create healthy boundaries that keep you distanced from those unable to fully appreciate and respect you! I'm not denying how challenging this can be, especially when we have so many degrading, depressing and devaluing ideas thrown at us about who we are and who we should be, but the bottom line is, we choose to be defined by someone else's opinions, OR we CAN choose to take the necessary actions toward our truth, our higher self, our love and our light. In order to shine to our brightest possible wattage, we must respect ourselves and others, but we will truly embark on a winning streak if we can combine this with focusing our attention on . . .

RESOLUTION:

In short, this simply means FORGIVE and stop punishing ourselves! Let me explain.

It's often comforting and feels safe to stay in the illusion of being stuck. We can become so accustomed to distress, that it actually seems easier to sit, dwell and moan about our problems and the pain caused to us by other people. But unfortunately this is eventually less productive than a mouse on a wheel, in a cage. If however, we can replace the word 'problem' with the word 'challenge', then it can instantly become a goal to be achieved, and believe it or not, we can grow in many magnificent ways. Of course, we are human and we have feelings and ego's to manage, and this can make it extremely difficult to see past our pain. But my gran always says, 'Wounds need to be aired in order to heal.' So find a person and place that you feel safe to vent, let it out and let it go, but with the intention of working towards a 'resolution.' Be sure to bless yourself with the ability to forgive others, no matter how impossible it may seem. Holding on to any resentment or thoughts of anger and disappointment for anyone, can only ever continue to hurt us.

People often tweet, retweet, post and repost slogans and self-development quotes about finding the strength, happiness and love WITHIN (me being one of them lol!), but there is much less information provided or made frequently available, teaching us HOW to find this connection WITHIN. So I do hope that the above has inspired you toward the first steps.

If nothing I've said has interested you or made any impact, perhaps simply sit and ask yourself the following 3 questions:

1. What stops me from being happy right now?

2. What can I do to change things? (What would I tell or do for my friends/family to help them achieve happiness, if they were me?) Make a plan.

3. Am I prepared to make those changes and give 'best friend' support to myself?

Everyone has experienced the pain and struggle within 'challenges' to some degree, and we will continue to do so until the day we part. It's good to try to remember that the difficult times will eventually pass, in the meantime, if we can start looking for all the reasons that we have to be thankful and happy, and attempt to stay focused on the positives, we can at least start to reduce and limit the amount of negativity we feel!

You are the ONLY you, and that is the MOST BEAUTIFUL thing about you, tell yourself that as often as you can, until you truly believe it and it becomes YOUR TRUTH!

Love, Light and Laughter!!

Niomi xxx

(Aka Ms. Dynamite)

KAREN BLACKETT

DEAR FRIEND

What an exciting time! You're at the beginning of such a fantastic journey. I have a few words of advice, which I hope can help you as you learn and grow and decide what your future will look like.

'You have two ears and one mouth, use them in that proportion,' is what my dad used to tell me. Always be open to learning. Listen to what your teachers say, your colleagues and your managers when you enter the workforce. Embrace lots of different stimuli, books and ideas, then figure out if there's an even better way to do things. There are so many great training programmes available for young people and work experience opportunities, it is a privilege to be able to participate and learn. Organisations such as Go Think Big are there to help you to navigate your future ambition. Learning doesn't stop either. Even when you're a CEO (if that's what you want to do), turn every opportunity into a learning experience.

It's really easy to say and more difficult to accept, but you really do need to be open to feedback and you have to seek it out. Achieving your goals happens when you open yourself up. You will never improve and become better unless you know what you're doing well and what can be done better. Some feedback you might find hard to accept, some feedback you might not want to hear. Some feedback you might not agree with, but perception is reality and you need to hear it. Cherish it and use it – good and bad.

'Celebrate your differences,' also rings loudly in my ears. You may look different and have a different background to other people in your school or college or even in the industry you decide to enter. Celebrate this. Do not change who you are to fit in. Authenticity is the key to success. Everybody is diverse and you can use your own unique insight and your background to bring diversity and relevance to what you do. Embrace your differences and avoid trying to 'cover' who you are.

Please remember to practice, practice, practice. The most accomplished people I have met in my career are those that fully prepare for presentations, meetings and events. They rehearse, know their craft and their content. Always train for the big meeting. Being clever is not enough. You have to really graft. Please be the hardest working and it will pay back. 'You're black and you're female, try twice as hard as anyone else.' Again wise words from my dad. Acknowledge the situation that you are in, but do not let it define you. Yes we are in a minority in the UK, yes you may not have all of the valuable connections that someone from a different background may have, but success is possible if you work hard and you believe it. Don't you dare have a chip on your shoulder, whinge about what has not happened or what is unfair. There are fabulous black female role models in the UK to prove that success is possible. Publications such as The Powerlist which detail Britain's most influential people of African and African Caribbean heritage prove what can be done with focus, belief and hard graft.

What really helped me during my career was to find a set of people who acted as my cheerleaders. These are people that will offer support and objective advice. You will experience highs and lows during your career. There will be challenges that at the time may look insurmountable, you may face periods of adversity or disappointment. I encourage you to seek out and find those people and organisations that will support you, give you objective advice and listen to you when you need them. They will champion you and help you to network. Everyone needs help and a guiding hand.

Let's be real. People can be incredible, generous and kind, but they can also be ignorant, selfish and cruel. I have experienced prejudice during my career. Thankfully, these occasions have been few and far between, but it does happen. How you deal with this is key. You will need to become resilient and learn not to take things personally. This doesn't mean that you need to become aggressive or cold to deal with these situations, quite the opposite. You deal with these situations with grace and kindness. I have been told during my career that someone didn't want to work with me because of my gender and skin colour. Did this upset me? Of course it did. Was I hurt? Of course I was. Would I want to work with someone that really thought like this? No, as I'd be miserable. There will be some situations that you cannot control or affect. Do not let these situations set you back or bring you down. Bounce back.

Perhaps the most important piece of advice I can give you is to surround yourself with brilliant, talented people. Make sure that the path you choose allows you this opportunity. Life is full of brilliant, inspiring people. Being part of a strong talented team will take you on an amazing path of discovery, excitement and learning. Enjoy every single minute of it!

Karen

KAY
OLDROYD

DEAR YOUNG WOMAN

You are enough.

Quite simply that means if you wipe off the labels that society wants to put on you by stepping out of the checkboxes that would have you defined according to your height; your weight; your skin colour your hair texture; your sexuality; your postcode; your mental health; your physical ability; your academic results; your taste in music; your language; your name. If you remove these labels you are all that you need to be for YOU.

In an age where technology and social media have made it so easy to connect with others yet become disconnected with ourselves, we as girls, young and older women have a constant reminder about how we should look and how we should be. But according to whom? Who has set this level of perfection and are we obliged to meet it?

Growing up, I did not have any belief in myself nor did I feel that I fit into this world. Statistically, coming from a low-income single parent household of mixed parentage with identity issues; experiencing racial bullying and isolation at school; being misunderstood and labelled within the education system leading to under-achievement and failing to attain a minimum of 5 GCSE's at A to C grade; drinking, smoking, staying out late and mixing with the wrong people to avoid the loneliness at home and to feel like I belonged; becoming a teenage mother and initially an embarrassment to my mother; on benefits and in social housing experiencing domestic violence and toxic relationships – statistically these circumstances should have had me following a path of failure.

And maybe for a while it looked that way.

I had no problems getting jobs. In my first

job at the age of 16, I became a civil servant in the very exciting role of issuing import certificates in the Department of Agriculture, Fisheries and Food. For a 16 year-old to be surrounded by 40 and 50 year olds who had been doing the same job for most of their lives I was sure it was a certain type of punishment! After about a year I walked out of there, much to my mother's annoyance and frustration at my lack of awareness about money and responsibilities. (I later wondered how I could have an awareness of something that I had never been taught.)

My employment career pretty much followed the same pattern throughout my teens, 20's and 30's – get a job, learn the ropes, be very good in the role, get bored. Move on. (I laugh now)*

Each time I would think to myself that there had to be something more than just going to work each day and doing 'stuff' just to fit in with the publicised normality of going to work Monday to Friday, living for the weekend and then repeating the cycle again.

When I hit the age of 30 I felt something amazing happen to me. I was empowered by the significance of the age and took great pride in telling people how old I was. When others were complaining about being 'old' I was rejoicing in the fact that I had reached a magical number (so I believed). I made some life-changing decisions and found a new person inside of me.

It took a few more years to discover my earthly purpose. But literally overnight my life was about to change. On the 12th of February 2008 I woke up in the middle of the night with a ridiculously strong vision and desire to create something. I don't mean like making a vase or painting a picture; I had been delivered a message that I was to create a legacy. As quickly as I had woken up, I went back to sleep again. Upon waking in the morning I instantly remembered what I thought had been a dream, but the clarity of this 'dream' did not leave me once I opened my eyes. In fact, it got stronger and stronger.

The short version of my story is that from 12th February 2008 to this present day I followed that dream. I created and have followed my own vision since, now running an award-winning company. I started with absolutely no structure or knowledge about what I wanted to do, armed only with ideas and passion. I share this part of my life with you so that you can maybe see that the over used saying of 'It's not where you've come from it's where you're going,' is actually very, very true and millions of people across the world would be able to tell you the same thing.

As a young woman growing up, what is most important is that you love yourself. Truly and deeply love who you are as a person. Appreciate that whatever mistakes you have made does not mean that you do not deserve to love yourself or be loved. You will not always get things right but at those times be open to learning the lesson that will be given.

Trust your instinct, that voice within that tells you when something doesn't feel right. When people or situations make us feel uncomfortable or scared, we should use our inner-wisdom that is there to guide us back out to safety.

Choose friends wisely. The people that you spend time with should be there to support you – not bring you down. They should inspire and uplift you – not encourage you to stand still.

The right friends are important and unlike family, we can choose them!

To my young sisters reading this, you are all you need to be for YOU. Each day is an opportunity to be a better version of you. Keep your dream alive and know that great power lies within you as a female. The media would have us to believe that we are just here to be sex objects online, in magazines, on billboards or in videos.

This is a great lie; as women we are the foundation of humankind and once you understand the true essence of feminine energy you will never underestimate yourself again.

So remember – you are enough. You have everything within you, so go out and be the best YOU that you can be.

Kay

*Note: I realised later on in life that it wasn't my fault (!). When I connected with my absent father around the age of 30 we had so much in common – especially his inability to stay in a job for much longer than 6 months, always getting new contracts, doing the work, and moving on. It's in the blood: nature vs. nurture.

MADELINE MCQUEEN

DEAR GIRLS,

I hope that you are well and more so I hope that you are embracing the magnificence that is within you.

I have daughters, and I have walked the road that you walk, especially in school where you are constantly battling to be seen, known and heard. I can remember one particular Valentine's Day hoping for a card from someone only to find that I had received none. Instead I found that the girls who looked nothing like me got them all.' This affected my view of how beautiful I truly was and it was not until I got older that I realised that my beauty was just as valid as any one of those other girls.

I tell my daughters daily that they are beautiful just the way they are, and so are you.

I firmly believe that we are all born magnificent. I want to encourage and empower you to be your best. I know that some of you may not often hear words that lift you up so I want to provide you with plenty of them. When you are at your best you are untouchable, you will feel great about yourself and find that you work smarter and more effectively. Many of us live our lives at half-mast, never realising our full potential.

I want you to know that you are beautiful just as you are. The hue of your skin is a delicious colour that is mesmerizing. Whether the sun shines or not you still have a skin tone that represents the sun. Never ever be negative about your beauty. Always remember that there are people who pay thousands of pounds in holidays and sunbeds to get a temporary version of your skin tone. This issue of dark and light skin and one being better than the other is a ploy to keep you stuck second guessing yourself and until you can see past these limiting thoughts you will not be able to achieve what you are capable of. Encourage yourself and your friends to see just how unique and beautiful the colour of your skin is.

Your hair is lovely, flexible and able to carry a range of styles that allow you to honour your heritage and your beauty. There is no such thing as 'good hair' – hair is hair! Do not allow yourself to feel intimidated or copy others just because their hair is a different texture to yours. You have the flexibility to wear your hair any way you want. There is a whole movement around natural hair online and offline; search out information about how you can manage what God has given you. You will find women of all shapes, sizes and colours enjoying the wonderful hair that they naturally have. Educate yourself about how to really care for your hair and your skin. There are many natural products that will make your skin and hair glow if you are willing to invest the time to get to know yourself better. You do not need to use someone else's hair or lighten your skin to prove your worth. You are enough and you are beautiful.

I asked my thirteen-year-old daughter what she felt I should say to you – this is what she said, 'Your hair and skin is beautiful but remember these do not determine your personality or who you are inside. There are many stereotypes out there but don't follow them or allow them to affect you. Push back and be yourself.' I couldn't have said it any better.

This is your life so ask for what you want; too often we live in fear and choose not to ask. Remember this: 'If you do not ask, the answer is always NO.' When you ask you have a 50% chance of a YES answer so please give it a go. The people in this life who get to where they want to be have overcome their fear of asking BY asking. The more you ask, the more you will get.

Believe in yourself and value yourself or no one else will; I have learned this the hard way. Your best supporter and your worst critic is you. We often spend our time waiting for someone else to notice us and to say that we have worth. Your value is held in your very own hands and no one else's. When you realise this, your belief in yourself will rise, you will value yourself more and you will quickly end relationships with people who use you. Self-belief is one of the keys to your success. There will be many obstacles in your way and people will tell you that you cannot achieve what you want to. If you focus on them you won't achieve anything. I encourage you to focus on what you know in your heart you are capable of. Ignore the naysayers; focus on being your best self.

One thing I tell my clients to do is to record their successes. Get a journal (a notebook) and write down all of the successes that you have had, no matter how big or small. You can also include kind words that people have said to you. Keep adding to your journal every time you have another achievement. Then on those days when your self-belief is low, go and look in your journal and you will be reminded of all of the successes that you have had. You will be surprised at how much this will boost your self-confidence and push you further towards achieving your dreams. It's hard to argue with evidence.

Go for what you want and focus in on it. Too often we let our dreams go because of someone else or because we are concerned about what others will think. Go for it. Work hard and work smart; effort is rewarded far more than talent. People who are successful have worked for what they want, not just hard but smart. They've invested in themselves, been hungry to learn and understand everything that they can about success and about their chosen field or industry. Be hungry for what you want and then focus in on it. Get really clear. Find out who the experts are in your chosen field of work and then see what they did to get to where they are.

You are capable and gifted. The only thing that stands between you and the success that you want is you. Are there obstacles along the way? Sure. Does racism rear its ugly head at times? Of course. But don't let these things or anything else stop you.

You are stronger than you believe and braver than you think, you have so much in you, so push for what you want. Focus and go for it. Believe in yourself and make it happen for you.

When you get to my age you realise that you have no one to blame but yourself. You either stand in the way of your success or you move out of the way and cheer yourself on.

You are a princess. A woman of worth, so honour yourself, take pride in yourself and hold your head up high. No one has the right to mistreat you. In a world that says that anything goes, hold on to your moral standards. You are not here for the use of people who do not respect you. Hold on to your self-respect and hold your NO. I know that for some young women many of the guys in your life expect you to be at their beck and call, delivering what is sacred and intimate on a silver platter for them. What you have is sacred, and anyone who does not respect that is not worthy of you.

There are so many pressures on you today to be what other people want you to be. Television programmes and celebrity culture promote an image that cannot always be recognised by us as black women and should not be copied. Do not fall into the trap of doing anything to be recognised, you don't need to, because when you are at your best that is enough. Remember, also, that you do not need anyone else to make you feel good about yourself. The answer to feeling great is not in a man or a bottle or in taking drugs. The answer is found in accepting yourself for who you are, working on being your best and taking action to achieve what you are capable of. Love yourself first and then you will find that the right people will love you.

No matter how hard you try there will always be people who will seek to stab you in the back or who will try to push their idea of who they think you are on to you. However, there will also be people who are supportive of you, people who provide wisdom and love. Learn the difference between these types of people and focus on those who want the best for you, not those who seek to use you for self-gain. We spend too much time trying to get people who do not like us, to like us. It's a waste of time. I encourage you to focus on those who love you, champion you and leave you feeling good about yourself.

One of my biggest learnings in life is to 'Do what I said I would.' We tend to talk about what we want to do and how we want our lives to be and do nothing to achieve it. Stop talking and start doing. Ask questions, learn, research and then take action. It is in taking action that things really change. Yes, I know that sometimes it can be frightening stepping out to achieve your goals and dreams but you have to just feel the fear and do it anyway. Fear can be crippling and can keep us stuck, however, we can use fear to move us forward and achieve so much more. I truly believe that by doing what we said we would do, facing our fears and taking action we can achieve great success. If you only ever talk about what you want to do, you will look around one day and find that talking was all that you did. So take action and make the life that you want your reality.

I have encouraged you to work hard and smart, but there is something else. Every life requires balance so go ahead and give yourself some chill-out time. Take time out to relax and recuperate. We have a legacy as black women of working ourselves into the ground, supporting everyone else and then when we look around we find that we are empty and have nothing left to give to ourselves. I have experienced burnout and it is not pretty; it leaves you feeling weak, helpless and exhausted. So take time out each month or week to do something just for you. Build it into your routine and you will find that it will help you to build the energy that you need to achieve your goals and more so you can build peace in your life.

Lastly, follow your intuition. You know, that voice inside that tells you what to do and what not to do, the inner feeling that is like a warning. That gut feeling that doesn't always have an explanation but it's often right. Listen to it. I have noticed that every time I do not listen I regret the choice that I made and every time I do listen it works out fine. It's not hocus-pocus, it's your inner being looking out for you.

Remember you are powerful, beautiful and wonderful, so, go ahead and grow a backbone of steel, focus on your dreams and do everything that you can to make them a reality. It is your life so live it well and remember: Be Magnificent!

Magnificently yours,

Madeline McQueen

JENNIFER GARRETT

DEAR SISTER,

If you identify with any of the below, you might be experiencing your teenage years with difficulty and the last thing that you need from me is ANOTHER lecture – I was a teen once too and I know what it's like:

Everyone tells you to grow up, but when you try they remind you that you're still a child

You wonder if anyone will ever fancy you, let alone find you to be 'The One.'

The images of beauty you see around you do not look like you, so where does that leave you?

Adults lecture and criticize and tell you that you need to work harder than everyone else

Friends, well they're the only ones who really understand and don't judge

So instead, let's think about you. Do you like music? Do you play it really loud in your bedroom? I want you to think of a black British female singer or vocalist, one that you like or can appreciate. I don't mind if it's Lil Simz, Emile Sande, Leona Lewis, Estelle or if the UK is too hard, you can swim across the waters and think of Rihanna, Nicki Minaj or Queen Bey. Whoever it is you identify with, it's all good.

Now keep in mind who you have chosen and tell me: Does she try to blend in? Does she try to fit in? Does she try to dull parts of her personality, intelligence and uniqueness to be liked? Do you think that she considers herself beautiful inside and out? Can you imagine Nicki Minaj saying, 'I just want people to like me and if that means I need to be someone else I'll do that?' No. Or, can you imagine Beyonce not being proud of her curves, worrying about having a thigh gap and being a size zero, or damaging her skin (that's probably insured for billions) with skin-lightening creams or self-harm. She wouldn't be her if she did that and she would actually be damaging her assets.

Their uniqueness and their pride in their own selves is what attracts us to them. They wouldn't be where they are today without embracing who they are, would they? They recognize that they are their own greatest asset and guess what. . . you are the same. A prized, precious, priceless jewel, maybe all you need is a little shine. Don't believe me? Don't do that very British thing and be all humble – lap it up, I mean it.

It can take time to know who you are, but those times when your friends make a joke and you're laughing on the outside but not on the inside, because the jokes on you, that's when you are not being you. Or those times when you have an uneasy feeling in your stomach because you know you shouldn't be doing something, or you are worried about being found out, that's when you are dulling your shine. But those times when you feel proud, you feel strong, in the words of Rihanna you 'shine bright like a diamond,' that's when you are really you!

The cosmetic industry would have you believe that beauty is an outside job, but it's really not true, it comes from within. That kind friend you have, doesn't she seem beautiful to you? That girl who has conventional beauty but is really mean, doesn't she seem ugly? Inner confidence and unconventional beauty, will take you much further than the other way around. Didn't you ever watch the TV show Ugly Betty? If not add it to your list now, to watch with your squad when you have your next sleepover.

Believe me we all make mistakes, but don't dwell on them, learn from them and move on. What's more important is to log the times when things go well for you, log them on your phone, remember them and find more times to feel like that. If you haven't experienced many, no problem. Seek out opportunities, try new things, and don't worry about what people think; you can be the first. Instead of being one of those people who say, 'Girls like me don't do things like that,' step out of the box that you and other people put yourself in. Look at the Williams sisters, black sisters excelling at tennis, who would have thought it!

So the next thing I am going to say, you're probably not going to like, but do you think that Lil Simz's first words out of her mouth was a rap and Emile Sande can just sing like that? Oh yes they're gifted, but gifts are wasted all the time, because they are not used. These women work hard at being better than they were. We all have gifts whether we know it or not, but more importantly we can all grow, YOU CAN GROW. What do I mean by that? Well if you want to be good at something you have to practice. You can't sit in front of the TV or on Instagram, go to sleep and expect to be better and more skilled in the morning; it is really not going to happen. There is no such thing as an overnight success.

Leona Lewis worked hard for years, working as a receptionist to get studio time to practice her music until she was discovered on the X-Factor. The preparation meant she was ready. If you want opportunities you too need to be ready. When you go to school and hand in your homework you may think that you are doing it for the teachers, or maybe your parents, or even the Government – you're not. You are doing it for you! It's all preparation so that when the opportunities come your way, you can grab them. School is the safest place to make mistakes, to try new things and to actually focus on learning. It may not feel like it, it may feel like they come down on you like a ton of bricks if you so much as forget your compass, but later on in life mistakes can cost you your job, your home, your car, and learning may be alongside many other commitments, maybe even babies. Enjoy preparing and practicing for the opportunities that will come your way. I saw a tweet recently 'ALL I WANT IS TO SLEEP FOR 2 YEARS AND WAKE UP WITH A DEGREE, AN APARTMENT AND MONEY IN THE BANK :')'

As I said earlier there are no shortcuts because you need to practice, but people can guide you to practice the right things. It can be hard to listen when every comment an adult makes sounds like a lecture, but guess why they're telling you? Because they don't want you to make the same mistakes. If you really want shortcuts to success, listen and learn and wake up to being successful. If someone's already done it, learn from them. You don't know it all, they don't know it all, but they know stuff you don't know. Drink it all up, what you don't need will disappear down the toilet as it does in life, but what you do need will stay with you.

I HAVE THREE CHALLENGES FOR YOU BEFORE SIGNING OFF:

1. Wake up to each new day excited for adventure as you never know what it will bring, who you'll meet, what you'll learn and what it will lead to.

2. Look at yourself in the mirror each day, look deep into those eyes and see your strength within. The strength of your heritage, your ancestors, and your faith and remember that they are always guiding you. Draw on this inner wisdom and walk tall.

3. Never let anyone put you in a box and don't put yourself in one either. I don't want to hear, 'I am the sporty one, so

I can't do . . .' You are anything you want to be, surprise them, shock them, make them eat their words.

Always know that I believe in you. You are more than enough.

Jenny

x

BIOGRAPHIES

TRICIA BAILEY

Tricia was born and raised in South-West London and is one of eight children.

Her interest in different languages and cultures caused her to excel in linguistics during her studies. Tricia's quest to be an inspiration and help others became apparent during her teenage years which resulted in her pursuing a career in all areas of administration.

Tricia has a passion and desire to see individuals utilise their innate gifts and talents while coming into their purpose and destiny. Tricia is an experienced Gospel singer and is honoured to have performed around the world at conferences and events. She is also the co-director of a graphic design company where she has the opportunity to interact with people from different industries and corporations.

As well as owning her own business, Tricia works at a Management Construction company in Beckenham, Kent on a part-time basis and is also involved in charity work.

Tricia's hobbies include fashion design, watching sports, music and creative writing. Her effervescent personality causes her to have great friends and to enjoy life to the full.

SINITTA

Sinitta is an American-born singer who has lived in the United Kingdom for most of her life. She is best known as a TV Personality and for her hit records in the 1980s including 'So Macho', 'Toy Boy', 'Cross My Broken Heart' and 'Right Back Where We Started From'. Altogether Sinitta has 14 international hit singles and three albums. She has also acted in a number of West End shows, been a mentor on The X Factor, and appeared as a contestant on the eleventh series of I'm a Celebrity . . . Get Me Out of Here! and the first series of Channel 4's The Jump, plus many more of our favourite TV shows.

Sinitta trained at the Legat Russian Ballet School, and at LAMDA (London Academy of

Music and Dramatic Art) which gave her the skills and discipline not only to be a performer but to keep herself in fantastic shape which she is asked to discuss on a regular basis.

Sinitta began in show business by appearing in the musical The Wiz and the movie Shock Treatment released on Halloween 1981. Her West End credits include Cats, Little Shop of Horrors, Smokey Joe's Cafe, Hair, Masquerade and Mutiny!

Sinitta continues to record and perform and also works with young talent, mentoring and spotting them for the music industry. She is also due to launch a new website sharing many of her fitness and beauty secrets and providing a unique retail environment.

JESSICA ELLIOTT

27 year-old Jessica Elliott is one of the UK's most visible young pioneers to have laughed in the face of rising unemployment figures and university debt to take control of her own financial future and become her own boss.

In 2007, aged just 20, Jessica founded J's Dance Factory with £200 and a dream. Months later Jessica's company provided dance classes in more than 25 schools across London with more than 1000 children, accessing classes on a weekly basis. The off-shoot JE Management, a talent agency for 2-17 year olds, has already seen Jessica's clients secure high profile roles in The Lion King, Matilda, BBC productions, and The Disney Channel to name a few. The school is currently being rolled out across the UK as a franchise.

Her dedicated work ethic and desire to make a social contribution have led to numerous awards including being listed on the Power List as a rising star and one of the most influential people of colour in the UK. Raised in Lewisham, South-East London by a single mother, Jessica was inspired by seeing her mother take pride in raising confident children with strong self esteem, to follow a similar path.

Jessica is being heralded as one of the UK's brightest entrepreneurial talents. A glistening role model for the next generation of how a recession or our economy need not determine one's future, Jessica's success is empowering for us all.

As one of the many awards that adorn her mantel exclaims, Jessica Elliott is absolutely one of 'London's top 10 people.'

RONKE LAWAL

Company founder Ronke Lawal was born in Hackney, East London of Nigerian parentage. Having graduated with honours from Lancaster University and the University of Richmond, Virginia (USA) with a degree in International Business (Economics), she started her own business in 2004.

In 2011 Ronke was honoured to receive a Precious Award for Inspirational Leadership. In January 2010, Ronke became the Chief Executive of the Islington Chamber of Commerce where she remained until the end of 2012 and became a non-executive director of The Hoxton Apprentice in 2011. She joined the board of Trustees of Voluntary Action Islington in 2012 where she is also a

Director of The Voluntary Action Academy and is currently on The Employers Panel for the National Employment Savings Trust. She is a mentor for The Cherie Blair Foundation and for The Elevation Network's Start Ups Initiative.

She is a passionate business woman running Ariatu Public Relations, a PR and marketing consultancy and the Simone Williams fashion label. Apart from her active business interests, her varied passions include food, travel, music, literature and most importantly living a life that she loves. Her love for food led her to create the 'Who's For Dinner?' food blog – www.whosfordinner.com.

Ronke's PR Services are geared towards many different business sectors and currently represent clients in various industries including entertainment, fashion, lifestyle and beauty, food and luxury goods. Ronke's company has a particular interest in businesses from the African /Caribbean Diaspora sector.

ANNMARIE LEWIS

Annmarie Lewis Mres, MA, BA Hons is the founding director of award-winning social enterprise Rainmakers Worldwide – turning yesterday's forgotten youth into today's entre-preneurs and tomorrow's world changers. She brings her person-centred approach to help shape youth, community work, social justice, practices and policy on an international scale. Annmarie is passionate about supporting people, which is evident through the hundreds of lives she has impacted both individually and corporately.

Her experiences include roles within the Prison Service; Youth Justice Board and London Youth, underpinned by her academic study. She is currently a doctoral student of Anthropology, focusing on transitional behaviours within a framework of criminality and entrepreneurship among young adults. Annmarie recently completed a Masters degree in Research, and also holds a Masters degree in Youth, Community Work and Applied Anthropology; a BA Specialist Honours degree in Criminal Justice Specialist (Juvenile Justice and Psychology) and numerous professional qualifications.

Annmarie is a qualified Action Learning facilitator, coach and mentor. Trained in advocacy and mediation she also runs a second consultancy delivering business coaching in capacity building; leadership training and development; change management; intra/entrepreneurship. Annmarie is a member of the Institute of Leadership and Management and a fellow of the School for Social Entrepreneurs.

Annmarie's life was completely transformed when she developed a personal relationship with Jesus Christ in 2006 and strongly believes that she is a living testament to the scriptures in Isaiah 6: 5-8; 61: 1-6 and Esther 4:

13-14. She works in a voluntary capacity in pastoral care, supporting local ministries and organisations within the wider voluntary and third-sector fields.

LEAH CHARLES-KING

Known for her vivacious character and engaging personality, the London-based presenter has approached a milestone of 15 years in the media and TV industry.

Leah Charles-King began her career as a child actress at the age of 5. Her television career started in 2001 as the first black female continuity Presenter on Children's ITV in its current 33-year history. Preceding this, Leah enjoyed 10 years in the music industry as a member of chart-selling girl-band, Kleshay eventually signed to Sony Music.

Leah has since presented and appeared in shows for ITV, BBC, The Disney Channel, Sky TV and more, including as a red carpet correspondent for international American network BET (Black Entertainment Television). The shows she has presented have been viewed in many regions including the UK and Europe, USA, Africa, the Middle East and the Caribbean, to a combined audience of over 90 million viewers.

Leah has enjoyed industry recognition by receiving the prestigious Screen Nation Award for Best Youth and Children's Presenter, and as the recipient of the 'Best Woman in Media' accolade from the Wise Women Foundation.

Leah recently launched The Red Carpet Academy. The UK's only TV Presenter and Public Speaking training academy led by mainstream and celebrity Experts!

Having many years experience as an accomplished entertainment presenter and public speaker, Leah is now combining her media skills with activism for women's empowerment and female social issues. This was inspired when she presented the making of 'Somebody Please (Help Haiti)', the remarkable project that brought together some of the world's most renowned gospel artists to raise money for the Haiti earthquake in 2010.

Amongst several television formats in development via her media company Princess King, Leah is currently involved in the production of a ground-breaking documentary entitled '(in) Visible Women' to highlight one of the most controversial issues at the heart of many western cultures: Is there a lack of women in visible areas of society such as the media, business, politics and others? The preview release has piqued worldwide interest.

By using her own experiences Leah hopes to empower and inspire young women who desire a career in the creative industries. She offers a number of limited internships within her own production company, Princess King Media and The Red Carpet Academy to provide an opportunity of work experience for students and graduates who are interested in the field.

CLAUDINE REID MBE

Voted as one of Britain's Top 100 Women Entrepreneurs by real business magazine in 2008, Claudine Reid MBE is considered to be one of the most inspirational women of our time. In addition to her role as Director of the award-winning Social Enterprise PJ's Community Service, providing services to enhance and transform communities through provision of care, education, economic empowerment, arts services and development programs, Claudine is a trainer, TV and Radio show presenter and Trustee for a London-based radio station.

Claudine's vast experience includes:

- Former Cabinet Office Social Enterprise Ambassador

- Appointment to the National Social Enterprise Expert Panel for the Government Office of Civil Society

- Panel member for the Prime Minister's Nomination Panel for the Big Society Awards

- Vice-Chair of Governors for a London Academy

- Former Chair of Governors for a London College for Girls

- Department for Works and Pensions – Ethnic Minority Advisory Board

- Co-Director of award-winning Social Enterprise established in 1992

ANGIE LE MAR

Angie Le Mar is a multi award-winning comedienne, businesswoman, speaker, writer, director, producer, talk show host and osargenews.com Brand Ambassador.

As one of Britain's top comediennes, Angie has successfully harnessed the power of laughter to create inspiring and thought-provoking productions. From stage, radio, TV and the written page Angie is a proven hit with a multicultural audience – male, female, young and old alike. She is equally at home with quick-fire comedy, acutely observed character sketches and solid acting performances.

Angie's wide-ranging career achievements, from being the first British performer to storm the legendary Harlem Apollo to making history in London's West End with the first ever sold-out show by a black comedienne, not only enables her to deliver top quality performance and production values on stage, screen and the airwaves, but also to attract a large and loyal fan base along with greatly increased audiences wherever her work appears.

As an Entrepreneur, Angie's aim is to inspire others to achieve against the odds and for two-and-a-half years she ran the Angie Le Mar School of expression fuelled by the desire to show young people not just show business, but the business behind it. It was a great success with a variety of special guests sharing their skills, including Jeffrey Daniels from Shalamar – who not only gave children advice but also taught them the famous Michael Jackson Moonwalk. Angie hopes re-open th school in the future.

Straight To Audience Productions is the company Angie founded in 2001 to build on her reputation as a performer and writer and also on her expertise in direction, production and marketing, serving the growing international market of vibrant and high quality black entertainment.

A guest appearance on ITV's Loose Women in 2012 inspired Angie to create an all female panel TV show called Ladies Talk to set a multicultural balance in today's media. The show had two successful runs, becoming an award-winning show on the Vox Africa Network.

BIANCA MILLER

After studying Business Management and Economics at the University of Sussex, Bianca joined the world's largest and most reputable management consulting and technology services firm. Whilst at Accenture, Bianca was HR advisor to a third of a thousand-strong graduate pool. In addition to her role she was asked by senior management to develop an initiative to help the graduates develop desirable skills to aid their career advancement. The initiative was called 'Preparing for Promotion.'

Bianca utilised her natural flair and like a duck to water began advising graduates of the of the personal brand attributes required to be successful. Having thoroughly enjoyed a career at Accenture, she felt it was time to move on and took a position at a reputable financial recruitment firm.

A brief stint in the world of recruitment enabled Bianca to experience first-hand the plight of unemployed individuals seeking employment in tough economic times.

When Bianca isn't running her business, facilitating workshops, networking or conducting meetings, she manages to find time to mentor students and is the ambassador for the Government flagship welfare to work scheme 'The New Enterprise Allowance'.

Bianca was a candidate on the BBC business show 'The Apprentice' in 2014, where she overcame tough competition to become the runner-up in the final of the show. Bianca's business idea is to launch a range of 'nude' hosiery for women of all ethnicities; from English Rose to Sub-Saharan African skin tones. She was piped to the winning post at the very last point. The final decision from Lord Sugar is still strongly contested by the media and fans of the show, but Bianca has persevered and intends to launch her tights 'Bianca Miller London' in the winter of 2015.

DR DIAHANNE RHINEY

Dr Diahanne Rhiney is a successful award-winning businesswoman with a proven track record in personal PR and reputation management. Her interview with the late Coretta Scott King was a poignant reminder of the courage and inner strength one person can pass on to another, together with the importance of empowering others and striving to achieve better.

As a leading consultant, Diahanne is a recognised and authoritative commentator on business-related success. She regularly speaks and presents at events, conferences and academic institutes. Her ability to inspire with a unique blend of authenticity, professionalism and humour resulted in one of her many accomplishments – hosting and commentating on Barack Obama's Inauguration Celebration in February 2009 followed by winning the Natwest Everywoman Athena Award in December 2009.

Diahanne is now the founder of The Rhiney Practice Group, which includes The Diahanne Rhiney Consultancy and The Practice of Change. Her consultancy is a cutting edge multi-faceted media production company that specialises in personal PR, personal branding, reputation management and TV. The Practice of Change deliver programmes that mentor and shape the next generation of leaders by providing the right environment for children and young people to access care and support.

Diahanne's experience also extends to counselling in areas such as domestic abuse (both physical and emotional) and has particular experience and passion when working with disenfranchised young people. She also champions young women affected by domestic violence and trauma.

SAMANTHA GOLDING

Born and raised in Birmingham, Samantha moved to London to study for her BA Hons in Business Studies.

Samantha has over 10 years' experience working in Operations Management, Finance and Events Management. Wanting to consolidate her skills and develop her career even further, in 2014, Samantha began to pursue her goal of becoming a School Business Manager. She is currently completing her Level 4 Diploma in School Business Management and is employed as an Office and Administration Manager at an Outstanding Primary Academy in South-East London.

Samantha is a firm believer that no goal is impossible to reach! Her optimism and positive approach to life is undergirded by her Christian faith. Renowned for her natural ability to motivate others, she is always readily available to provide counsel and mentorship to women of all ages and from all walks of life.

Samantha is married to Julian and they have two children.

JENNI STEELE

Jenni Steele has spent the past 10 years building a career dedicated to celebrating inspirational people. She began with mentoring young people and providing a platform for female entrepreneurs to network and now has her feet firmly planted in Media after creating her popular show 'Keeping It Real with Jenni Steele.' Jenni created the 'Keeping It Real' brand to inspire and motivate her audience by celebrating local Heroes and She-roes with real stories of overcoming adversity and forging into entrepreneurship and success. In 2014 she added the 'Keeping It Real Lifestyle' show to her repertoire; incorporating the beauty, fashion and entertainment industries.

The 'Lioness Ladies Women's Network' was founded in 2010, a monthly event for women to promote or showcase talents, bringing together professional women and potential entrepreneurs.

The Keeping it Real with Jenni Steele Show launched online in 2013. Jenni interviewed amazing people weekly about their lives and was soon inundated with guests from all over the UK with some international guests being interviewed via telephone.

In 2014 Jenni shared a very personal story by revealing that she was physically abused by a boyfriend at age 16 and almost died. She became the National Ambassador for Domestic Violence UK and helped to launch their 'Love Doesn't Hurt' Campaign in Westfield London with Strictly Come Dancing stars Janette Manrara and Aljaz Skorjanec.

Today, Jenni Steele is a broadcast journalist, motivational speaker, mentor and founder of The Jenni Steele Foundation, which helps young people to fulfil their dreams and give them the motivation they need to plan a successful future.

MS. DYNAMITE

Niomi Arleen McLean-Daley, better known as Ms. Dynamite, is a hip-hop and R&B recording artist, rapper, songwriter, and record producer. She is the recipient of the Mercury Music Prize, two BRIT Awards and three MOBO Awards.

KAREN BLACKETT

Karen has been in the Media industry for 20 years, currently running the largest media agency in the UK, MediaCom. In her role as CEO, Karen controls £1.2bn of media billings, manages over a thousand people and in 2014 led the agency to acquire over £119m of new business. Karen has also been personally recognised in the industry, featuring twice in Management Today's 35 Under 35, and five times on the Power List of the UK's 100 most influential black people – most recently this year, where she came in at number 1. In 2012 Karen launched an apprentice scheme encouraging young people from all backgrounds to get a foot in the door of the industry. She is also a Trustee of a charity named Adopt a Better Way and was one of the finalists in the Veuve Cliquot Business Women awards 2014. In June 2014 Karen received an OBE in the Queen's Birthday honours for services to Media and Communications.

KAY OLDROYD

Kay Oldroyd is the founder and director of Youth in Excellence CIC (YiE); a social enterprise that works with young people, families, schools and communities in a way that promotes understanding, confidence, empowerment and progression through a range of products and services.

Youth in Excellence run the annual Black Youth Achievement Awards – a national cere-mony that celebrates and promotes the diversity and accomplishments of young people from around the UK across various categories.

Kay started the BYA Awards in 2008 and since then the movement has recognised over 300 individuals and nurtured a number of achievers through building partnerships with major organisations such as Microsoft, British Council, Barnardo's, Channel 4, University of Sussex, Pearson PLC, Hewlett Packard, Legal and General, BITC (Business in the Community) and Crystal Palace FC Foundation. 910 Publishing sponsored the Literary Arts category in 2014. Nominations for awards are open until 31st August, see www.bya-awards.com

Kay has over 20 years' experience of help-ing people in a variety of roles, starting with young children in nursery and primary schools to supporting victims of domestic violence; advising and guiding clients back into work; mentoring and coaching students in further education and supporting students who have been excluded from mainstream education due to a myriad of complex issues ranging from low self-esteem and confidence, drugs, neglect, abuse (sexual, physical, emotional and men-tal), prostitution and gang activity. Kay has organised and facilitated family forums, where children and parents come together to discuss and tackle a range of issues that are affecting them. Kay also offers mentoring to women who want to set up their own social enterprise but may lack the confidence, support or knowledge in doing so.

Kay's work has been recognised at the Mayor of London's Peace Week in 2010 where she collected the Volunteer of the Year Award and she was also named one of Europe's Most Powerful Black Women, along with earning herself a place in the Black 100+ Legacy Book in the same year. In 2014 Kay was a finalist at the National Diversity Awards.

MADELINE MCQUEEN

Madeline McQueen is a woman who is passionate about empowering others to be their best. She is the wife of David McQueen, mother to two beautiful daughters and the youngest of six sisters. She firmly believes that life is a journey and the experiences encountered show you how to navigate it. She has had her fair share of ups and downs but her mission is simple, to get the people she works with from where they are now to where they want to be.

Madeline has a proven track record of success that spans over twenty years in coaching, consulting, sales and running businesses. She started running her first business with her husband in 2004. She now runs Magnificent Generation, a training company for young people and Madeline McQueen Ltd, a coaching and consulting practice. She is a sought after professional speaker. Madeline is also a Trustee for Hestia, a charity that supports those on the fringes of society.

Madeline firmly believes that when we feel empowered and confident we are then able to have a positive impact on our society and our own lives.

JENNIFER GARRETT

Jenny started her life from humble beginnings, born to a teenage mother and spending her first years on a London council estate. Jenny wanted to study art when she left school but was not able to get a grant at the time. Instead she studied part-time in the evening for 5 years to get her degree. She worked her way up to Marketing Director before being introduced to coaching by a colleague and then embarking on running her own business.

Jenny is the author of Rocking Your Role, a how-to guide to success for female breadwinners. Since the publishing of her book, Jenny has worked hard to share the Rocking Your Role message in the UK, Spain, Botswana and the US to name a few of the countries where she has provided talks that enable her audience to gain a better understanding of their life situations and how to make things happen, their way.

Jenny Garrett is now an award-winning coach and founder of Reflexion Associates, a leadership and coaching consultancy. She is also the creator of the online coaching programme, the Happenista Project and co-founder of Rocking Ur Teens CIC.

CONTRIBUTOR CONTACT DETAILS

ANGIE LE MAR

W: www.angielemar.com

T: @angielemar

FB: www.facebook.com/pages/
Angie-Le-Mar-Fan-Page/188796717815910

I: angielemar

ANNMARIE LEWIS

W: www.rainmakersworldwide.org.uk

E: info@rainmakersworldwide.org.uk

T: @rainmakersww

FB: www.facebook.com/RainmakersWW

BIANCA MILLER

W: www.the-be-group.com

E: info@the-be-group.com

T: @TheBeGroup1
@Bianca_B_Miller

P: 0208 667 9519

FB: www.facebook.com/TheBeGroup1

L: www.linkedin.com/in/biancamiller

CLAUDINE REID

W: www.claudinereid.co.uk

E: admin@claudinereid.co.uk

T: @claudinereid1

P: 020 8239 6911

FB: www.facebook.com/claudine.reid.54

DIAHANNE RHINEY

W: www.diahannerhiney.com

E: hello@diahannerhiney.com

T: @diahanneuk

P: 020 3474 0123

FB: facebook.com/diahanne

I: diahanneuk

JESSICA ELLIOT

W: www.Jsdancefactory.co.uk
www.jessicaelliottmanagement.com

E: jessica@jessiaelliottmanagement.com

T: @jsdancefactory

P: 0844 414 2755

FB: www.facebook.com/pages/
Js-Dance-Factory/22797341466

I: @jsdancefactory

JENNIFER GARRETT

W: www.rockingyourrole.com

E: jenny@reflexion-uk.co.uk

T: @JenniferGarrett

P: + 44 (0)844 776 4744

FB: www.facebook.com/Reflexion.Associates

I: rockingyourrole/

L: www.linkedin.com/in/jennygarrettreflexion

JENNI STEELE

W: www.JenniSteele.net

E: jenni@jennisteele.net

T: @OfficialJenniSteele

FB: www.facebook.com/
KeepingItRealWithJenniSteele

I: @OfficialJenniSteele

CONTACT NUMBERS FOR SUPPORT

- 24-hour National Domestic Violence Freephone Helpline for women 0808 2000 247

- www.TheHideout.org.uk is a safe website for teenagers and fully confidential.

- www.DVUK.org has a directory that can put in the direction of services in your or your friends local area.

KAREN BLACKETT

W: www.mediacomuk.com

T: @ blackett_kt

FB: www.facebook.com/MediaComGlobalNews

L: www.linkedin.com/in/blackettk

KAY OLDROYD

W: http://youthinexcellence.com

E: kayoldroyd@youthinexcellence.com

T: YIExcellence

FB: www.facebook.com/YIExcellence

LEAH CHARLES-KING

W: www.leahcharlesking.co.uk

T: @leahcharlesking

I: leahcharlesking

MADELINE MCQUEEN

W: www.madelinemcqueen.com

E: info@madelinemcqueen.com

T: @madelinemcqueen

P: 0203 137 9533

MS DYNAMITE

W: http://www.msdynamite.co.uk

T: @ms_dynamite

FB: www.facebook.com/msdynamiteofficial

RONKE LAWAL

W: www.ariatupublicrelations.com

T: @ronkelawal

L: www.linkedin.com/in/ronkelawal

SINNITA

W: www.sinitta.com

T: @sinittaofficial

I: thesinittaofficial

TRICIA BAILEY

W: www.kairossolutions.com

T: @kairossolutions

FB: www.facebook.com/kairosdesignsolutions

Have you read...

LETTERS TO A
YOUNG
GENERATION

13 inspirational letters to
the next generation of men

FOREWORD BY ROUGH COPY
EDITED BY AMANDA WILSON